T0356399

The Good, the Bad, and the Emoji

The Good, the Bad, and the Emoji

Mastering the Art of Review Data

Menno Beker, Hans Keukenschrijver,
and Wouter Hensens

BUSINESS EXPERT PRESS

Leader in applied, concise business books

The Good, The Bad, and The Emoji: Mastering the Art of Review Data

Copyright © Business Expert Press, LLC, 2025

Cover design by Raimond Hof – www.hofcommunicatie.nl

Interior design by Exeter Premedia Services Private Ltd., Chennai, India

All rights reserved. No part of this publication may be reproduced, stored in a retrieval system, or transmitted in any form or by any means—electronic, mechanical, photocopy, recording, or any other except for brief quotations, not to exceed 400 words, without the prior permission of the publisher.

First published in 2024 by
Business Expert Press, LLC
222 East 46th Street, New York, NY 10017
www.businessexpertpress.com

ISBN-13: 978-1-63742-704-0 (paperback)
ISBN-13: 978-1-63742-705-7 (e-book)

Business Expert Press Tourism and Hospitality Management Collection

First edition: 2024

10 9 8 7 6 5 4 3 2 1

Description

Prepare yourself for an immersive journey into the digital landscape of customer feedback mastery with *The Good, the Bad, and the Emoji: Mastering the Art of Review Data.*

Authored by online review entrepreneurs Menno Beker and Hans Keukenschrijver, alongside hospitality expert Dr. Wouter Hensens, this groundbreaking book reveals the secrets to harnessing online reviews' power to influence consumer behavior, foster trust, and product success.

Drawing from over two decades of expertise, development, and real-world encounters, this dynamic trio has curated a comprehensive yet accessible toolkit for navigating the world of customer feedback. From demystifying various review data sources to leveraging state-of-the-art AI technologies, this book empowers everybody with indispensable insights crucial for thriving in today's digital era.

The Good, the Bad, and the Emoji stands as your indispensable companion in conquering the realm of online reviews and safeguarding the future of your organization.

Keywords

how to manage reviews; how to analyze reviews; how to get reviews; how to interpret reviews; review customer service; review marketing; digital marketing reviews; review management; trends in review analysis; artificial intelligence in reviews; strategic use of online feedback; marketing strategies with review data

Contents

Testimonials

Accor

"Having easy access to the web has radically changed the way people shop for almost everything today. In the hotel industry, we recognise that it is rare for our potential guests to blindly make a purchase decision without reading through several online reviews, whether this be via Trip Advisor, Google hotel listing, Instagram or travel blogs. In fact we have seen in a recent study that more than 65% of travelers trust others experiences more than any marketing material provided by hotels.

Online reviews provide a wealth of consumer data and represent a window to the world, essentially to attract and maintain loyal customers across all digital touch points.

Hotel organisations need to be future focussed and ensure that they are recruiting and skilling talent within their teams to drive business through online channels and have the adequate knowledge, technology and resources to manage their online reputation in this ever growing world of digital marketing. This book provides a much needed resource in this regard."—**Debbie Simister, Global VP Talent Management, Accor**

Cloudbeds

"If I have a question about review marketing, I call Hans and Menno. The Good, the Bad and the Emoji *provides a clear roadmap for navigating and harnessing the power of online reviews, giving any hotelier a significant market advantage. This is a vital read for those ready to adapt to the changing review landscape and find sustainable success.*"—**Adam Harris, Cofounder and CEO of Cloudbeds**

Rabobank

"Market sentiments play an essential role in the current and future valuations of real estate properties. The reputation of business owners and operators

cannot be ignored in today's valuation models, especially for exploitation driven objects. This book is an essential guide for real estate experts, providing valuable insights into leveraging the power of online reviews, data and analytics."
—Roel van de Bilt, Board member, Rabobank Real Estate Finance

The Mantis Collection

"Throughout my 30-year journey in the industry, I've witnessed the evolution of marketing, with a particular emphasis on Guest Reviews in the Boutique Industry. From the early days of relying on celebrity endorsements to the present era of electronic 'Word of Mouth,' one thing remains unchanged—the significance of our valued guests.

In this digital age, we must embrace the reach and influence of online platforms, but never forget the importance of our guests—the heartbeat of our industry. For anyone seeking insights into the transformative role of Guest Reviews in the Hospitality Industry, this story is a must-read."—**Adrian Gardiner, Founder and Executive Chairman, The Mantis Collection**

Reviews From Readers

"Menno, Hans and Wouter highlight the subject with practical use-cases. Their approach not only makes the subject clear and easy to follow, but also gives readers concrete examples. They have made a daunting topic accessible to a wide audience. Clear, well structured, and directly useable book in practice."
—M. V Bekkum | September 19, 2023

"From the very first page of The Good, the Bad, and the Emoji *you are drawn into the epic story of David and Goliath. The title, with its mix of humor and depth, is just the beginning of what this book has to offer.*

Within our organization at Postillion Hotels, we invariably believe in the essential importance of feedback and customer experience. This book illustrates exactly why this is so fundamental in the current business context. Hans, Wouter and Menno have delivered a formidable achievement by composing this book that goes beyond mere theories. They offer hands-on examples and practice-oriented use-cases that are immediately applicable in the real world.

The part of the book that explains how organizational improvements can be made was enlightening. But if a minus should be noted, it is that the book may at times be a bit technical for newcomers to this domain. That said, for anyone with some knowledge of customer service and feedback systems, this book is a gold mine of insights.

In short, The Good, the Bad, and the Emoji *is mandatory reading for those who really want to take the customer feedback in their organization to heart and get started with it."*—**B. van der Heide | September 25, 2023**

"Not easy to capture the entire framework of review data in relatively simple concepts. Menno, Hans and Wouter have succeeded in unlocking the key concepts, applications and functions of review data in a practical way from a to z, with very practical examples to actually get started with making these unique sources of information "actionable.""—**L. G. J. van den Oever | October 18, 2023**

"This book about reviews is in-depth and yet extremely accessible, and definitely deserves a review.

The book offers an enjoyable combination of inspiring examples, such as why hotel rankings are no longer dominated by chains, to in-depth insights into collecting and analyzing reviews, including explaining how web scrapers work. In addition, the book contains inspiring examples from hospitality and e-commerce. It explains in an understandable way how the power of reviews works and how David can beat Goliath with it."—**R. de Bruyn | October 8, 2023**

"In today's world, where information is spread at lightning speed through digital channels, reputation management is invaluable. Reviews play a crucial role in this. The book The Good, the Bad and the Emoji *offers an enlightening and inspiring journey through this complex and crucial area."*
—**N. P. Bronsvoort | October 3, 2023**

Disclaimer

The information provided in this book is for general informational purposes only. The author and publisher make no representations or warranties of any kind, express or implied, about the completeness, accuracy, reliability, suitability, or availability of the information contained herein. Any reliance you place on such information is strictly at your own risk.

The content of this book is not intended to be a substitute for professional business advice. Always seek the advice of a qualified business professional or consultant regarding any specific questions or concerns you may have. The author and publisher disclaim any liability or responsibility for any loss or damage incurred by readers or users of this book, directly or indirectly, arising from the use or application of any information provided within.

While the authors and publisher have made every effort to ensure that the information presented in this book is accurate and up to date at the time of publication, they make no representations or warranties of any kind, express or implied, about the completeness, accuracy, reliability, suitability, or availability of the information, products, services, or related graphics contained in this book for any purpose. Any reliance you place on such information is strictly at your own risk.

The mention of specific companies, products, or services in this book does not imply endorsement or recommendation by the author and publisher unless explicitly stated. Similarly, the omission of any particular company, product, or service should not be construed as a negative judgment or evaluation.

The author and publisher shall not be liable for any direct, indirect, incidental, consequential, or special damages arising out of or in any way connected with the use of this book or the information contained herein, whether based on contract, tort, strict liability, or other legal or equitable theory, even if advised of the possibility of such damages. Every effort has been made to accurately represent the strategies, concepts, and techniques discussed in this book. However, the effectiveness of these strategies may vary depending on individual circumstances and market conditions. The author and publisher do not guarantee or warrant any specific results or outcomes as a result of applying the information provided in this book.

All trademarks, service marks, trade names, product names, and logos mentioned in this book are the property of their respective owners and are used for identification purposes only. Use of these names, trademarks, and brands does not imply endorsement.

Any links, references, or resources provided in this book are for informational purposes only. The author and publisher do not have control over the content, availability, or accuracy of external websites, resources, or services. The inclusion of any links, references, or resources does not necessarily imply a recommendation or endorsement.

Readers are encouraged to conduct their own due diligence and research before making any business decisions or implementing any strategies discussed in this book. By reading this book, you acknowledge and agree to the above disclaimers and limitations of liability. Please note that there may be occasional errors or inaccuracies in the English language, and we apologize if anyone feels offended.

Reviews are the currency of the digital age, they can mean the difference between a thriving industry and a struggling one. By embracing review marketing, we can harness the power of customer feedback to build trust, enhance our reputation, and ultimately attract more visitors.

—Menno Beker, Hans Keukenschrijver, and Wouter Hensens

Acknowledgments

We would like to express our heartfelt gratitude to all the readers who have supported us throughout the journey of writing this book. Your interest and enthusiasm have been a tremendous source of motivation for us. We are deeply thankful to everyone who contributed to this book. Without your help, this book would not have been possible.

Special thanks to Raimond Hof of Hofcommunicatie for all his hard work, and to Geert Jan Hoogeslag of UWKM. Your invaluable contributions have been instrumental in making this book a reality. And of course, a special thanks to Robert Bishop for his invaluable assistance with this book.

We thank you, dear reader, for exploring this exciting new field with us. We hope this book will increase your knowledge and provide you with new perspectives on the subject. We would love to hear your thoughts and feedback, so please do not hesitate to reach out!

Hans, Menno, and Wouter

Introduction

In today's fast-paced, interconnected world, customer feedback has become more important than ever. Reviews have the power to shape consumer behavior, build trust, and ultimately determine the success of a product or service. With the proliferation of digital platforms and the increasing influence of social media, the volume and variety of review data available have grown exponentially, providing businesses and consumers with unprecedented access to insights and information. In this book, we explore the fascinating world of review data, from its evolution from word of mouth to sophisticated online platforms, and its far-reaching impact on businesses, consumers, and industries.

We first explore the phenomena of small hotels outperforming larger international hotel brands and how this can be in Chapter 1. The principles here apply way beyond small hotels and teach us the key mechanisms of receiving great online reviews. In Chapter 2, we explore this further as we link service excellence and customer engagement with online review marketing, arguing that you cannot market yourself out of a poor service delivery.

In Chapters 3 and 4, we tackle online review data collection and analysis practices and techniques. Where and how do you collect data, clean it, and store it for analysis? What techniques can you then use to analyze your data and what does this tell you?

In Chapter 5, we really enter the space of online review marketing. We outline what the data does and does not tell us and how we can use it to our benefit in order to better our product and service concept, our market positioning, and authentic marketing communication. We then explore the concept and practices of customer engagement marketing and how we can use online review data for successful pricing strategies and revenue management. We close off the chapter by exploring the economy of trust and what this means as we seek to optimize our online reputation.

In Chapter 6, we look at how AI can help us to more efficiently and effectively collect, analyze, and manage online reviews. We also take a future look into what awaits us as AI becomes more readily available in different industries.

We conclude this book with practical tips and tricks to use online review data and build a comprehensive review data strategy and provide some helpful references of leading platforms that may assist you in your journey.

We hope you enjoy reading this book as much as we have enjoyed writing it and we look forward to hearing your feedback.

Hans, Menno, and Wouter

CHAPTER 1

The New Marketing Paradigm

How David Takes on Goliath

Unless you have 100% customer satisfaction you must improve.
—Horst Schulze Ritz-Carlton

If David and Goliath Were Hotels

The story of David and Goliath inspires us. It reminds us that the smaller, weaker opponent does not always have to lose. Through courage or belief or simply by working harder or smarter, David can win.

The story of David and Goliath is a perfect metaphor for how online guest reviews have provided a sling to small unbranded hotels as they try to compete in the luxury hotel segment with established global hotel brands in markets all over the world. Prior to online guest reviews, the Davids of this world had little chance of competing successfully against the much bigger and better-resourced global hotel giants. Their marketing budgets were nonexistent, their distribution channels were limited, and they were not appealing for tour operators who were looking for volume and brand recognition. Today, this picture has changed radically and one could argue that the playing field has been leveled.

In this introduction, we seek to explore how online guest reviews have changed our perception of quality in hotels and what this means for small independent hotels as they compete in global markets. These changes are not unique to the hospitality industry, as the rise of online reviews has disrupted and changed each industry dealing directly with consumers, as we will highlight throughout this book. The hotel sector in particular provides excellent insights into the dynamics at play.

Figure 1.1 David and Goliath

A New Quality Paradigm for Hotels

The 1980s gave rise to new ideas on how we measure the quality of services. The realization that conventional quality management techniques for tangible products were not suitable for measuring service quality resulted in a new approach to service quality management. This approach focused on meeting customer expectations rather than fixed features on what a service should look like. This was followed by the idea that service quality is based on satisfaction not just with the service itself, but also with the entire service delivery process and customer experience. These insights continue to influence the way businesses approach customer service and quality management today.

Up to that point, the hospitality industry measured quality as something that was to be ascertained by experts who would very often focus on tangible elements of a hotel to establish its classification (one to five stars) or its compliance to a brand standard. Guests would navigate their hotel selection based on these star ratings or brand, as they had no other way of determining what quality they could expect as they selected a hotel. The process of booking a hotel stay is quite unique in that we typically do not have the means to visit it prior to our booking and therefore we have to rely on indirect sources.

This gave hotels a lot of space to overpromise their offerings and secure bookings. Sometimes this was subtle—by using a wide-angled lens to make rooms appear more spacious—and sometimes shamelessly, by promising facilities and services that were simply not being offered. Hotel rating systems and international hotel brands provided some assurance of the standards and quality that one could expect; however, neither was close to perfect. Hotel classification systems would be limited to a hotel classification inspector's interpretation of the infrastructure of the hotel and comprise a snapshot that would take place once a year at best. International hotel brands would typically be able to ensure a consistent standard of hotel infrastructure, but, in terms of upkeep and daily service delivery, would not always deliver as per standard.

Alec Le Sueur's book *Hotel on Top of the World* proves this point as he chronicles his experiences in the five-star Yak and Yeti hotel in Kathmandu, Nepal, from 1985 to 1991 in a hilarious manner. The hotel was managed by the Golden Tulip, which had taken over the management of the hotel from Sheraton. La Sueur writes about the challenges that arose during the initial opening of the Yak and Yeti hotel and how he was responsible for ensuring that all aspects of the hotel were operational. He describes how the hotel had been constructed over 20 years earlier and some aspects of it were outdated, including the locking system for the rooms. He writes:

> *I discovered that all the room keys were the same, and therefore the system was useless. Any key would open any room. It was like a credit card belt that had been bought for a rupee at a market stall.*

Le Sueur's memoir confirms the point that neither a five-star rating nor an international brand was guarantee for an uneventful stay, especially in developing markets. However, even in more developed markets with more rigid and more frequently controlled standards, a star rating or an international brand did not guarantee a positive guest experience simply because of the limited scope and perhaps the paradigm by which quality was measured.

The launch of TripAdvisor in 2000 marked the beginning of a radical change in how we view quality in hotels. No longer were expert inspectors or international hotel brands the judges for what can be considered a great hotel; it was the actual guests. From 2007 onward, TripAdvisor's popularity and widespread use has grown exponentially from 4 million reviews in 2007 to 25 million reviews in 2010 and over 1 billion in 2023. The first decade of TripAdvisor's existence was marked by questions about the reliability of its reviews. How could we know they are real and not written by the hotel itself? Or its angry competitor? Discussions also revolved around the objectivity of hotel guests: "Are they not subjective in their opinions?" Both arguments were flushed out as the volume of reviews started to run in the hundreds and even thousands for a single hotel. It became rapidly clear that it would simply not be possible to falsify that volume of reviews, especially with TripAdvisor's algorithms screening the user accounts and IP addresses as well as some very clever-wording checks. It also became clear that travelers were quite comfortable to rely on the subjective opinions of hundreds of peers as opposed to that of one expert hotel inspector. With Booking. com, Expedia.com, and many other online travel agents following suit in publishing verified online guest reviews, the argument was settled that indeed the guests decide what constitutes quality in hotels.

Today, we can comfortably book a hotel on the other side of the world that does not feature an official star rating or an affiliation to a global brand. We visit one or more online guest review platforms, look at the scores, read a few reviews, and feel comfortable that our experience will be similar to those that went before us.

The TripAdvisor Top 10

Between 2009 and 2011, we conducted our first research into online reviews. We looked for identifying traits of the top 10 ranked hotels on TripAdvisor in 11 large cities across the world, starting in Amsterdam. We expected to see mostly international hotel brands comprising 300-bedroom five-star branded hotel properties with formal structures, training, departments, and protocols. This was, in our training, the model that should achieve the highest standards and should therefore yield the highest guest review scores.

None of these five-star branded hotels that we knew or had worked with featured in the TripAdvisor's top 10 in 2009. What was worse, we did not recognize a single hotel in the top 10!

As we went on to analyze the list, we learned that only two hotels in the list featured more than 100 rooms and belonged to an international brand. The average hotel in the top 10 featured only 55 rooms and the top 3 averaged less than 8 rooms. Revisiting this list in 2023, we noted that some of the names have changed, but the trend has not. Only 3 out of the 10 leading hotels in Amsterdam on TripAdvisor represent hotels that belong to a brand, only 1 has more than 100 rooms, and the average size is 53 rooms.

This observation is not limited to Amsterdam. It can be observed in many other tourism destinations: the top hotels seem to be small, independent, and quite frequently owner-managed.

Why is this? Don't larger and internationally affiliated hotels have many more resources to deliver exceptional service and an unforgettable stay? There is no argument that larger hotels benefit from economies of scale and should be able to offer more facilities and services to their guests from the simple observation that the costs of these additional services and facilities could be absorbed by more rooms. They typically also have the benefit of better technology, standardized processes, centralized support structures, guest loyalty schemes, and many other advantages that small independent hotels do not have.

However, there is one critical thing that large hotels typically struggle with and that is *personalization*. Guests want to be catered to their personal needs and not to a general standard. They want to be recognized, engaged with, and referred to as a unique individual with unique needs during their stay. These needs can only really be catered for in a small-scale service setting where the host gets to know the guest and his or her unique needs. A simple example is that of coffee choice at breakfast. Let's say a guest likes to drink a double espresso first thing in the morning before even ordering breakfast. In a boutique hotel, this is noted on the first morning and, from thereon, built in as a routine, very often without the waiter even asking. This makes a guest feel recognized and special: "the waiter knows who I am and what I like." This cannot possibly be replicated in even the most luxurious 400-room five-star hotel unless supported by technology or dedicated butlers on each floor. The first solution would probably not be perceived as real, and the second one would escalate the cost of stay to only be accessible for the lucky few.

Especially when it comes to unique travel needs, small independent hotels find themselves in a position to exceed expectations more easily—from hosts getting up outside of normal times to prepare breakfast for guests who need to depart early to tailored food and drink presentations in the room, to unique travel advice. This kind of service delivery results in ratings and results that allow these small hotels to dominate the top places on online review platforms.

The Marketing Advantage

There is a strong positive relation between online review ratings and the financial performance of a hotel. Studies have found that hotels with higher online review ratings report higher occupancy rates, higher room rates, and higher revenue per available room (RevPAR) compared to those with lower ratings. A 1 percent increase in a hotel's average online review rating on websites like TripAdvisor can lead to a 1.42 percent increase in RevPAR[1].

Other studies have consistently found that higher online review ratings lead to higher hotel prices and increased occupancy rates, which mean that guests are willing to pay more for hotels with better reputations. These findings indicate that online review ratings should be a priority for hotels as they ultimately drive financial performance.

This, however, also works the other way around: while marketing can help to promote a hotel and increase its visibility, it is unlikely to be enough to overcome consistently negative online reviews. Marketing can attract new guests to a hotel, but once they begin reading negative reviews about the property, they will be hesitant to book a stay.

TripAdvisor finds that 97 percent of travelers in the United States consider online reviews important when choosing a hotel for their next trip and 85 percent of travelers worldwide think reviews are essential in the decision-making process, with 79 percent indicating that they are more likely to book a hotel with a higher rating[2].

In other words, a great hotel that consistently receives excellent scores will have to do very little marketing, and a hotel that consistently receives poor reviews cannot possibly "market" its way out of that poor reputation. The differentiating factor in terms of competitive advantage is therefore

not in how well one can position oneself, but what one's guests have to say about the hotel. The data are clear that smaller and independently owned hotels have the edge to dominate the top of the charts and from that position beat Goliath.

How Do They Do It?

But, exactly, how does this work? What are these top-performing small hotels doing that makes guest rate them a 10 out of 10 instead of, say, an 8 or a 9 out of 10? Besides not disappointing the guest, which is an obvious requirement, the top-performing hotels "delight" the guests, that is, they exceed expectations to a point of surprise and delight. This can happen in different ways but typically would revolve around staff going beyond what is expected as they assist with unique guest challenges and needs, upgrades or discounts, and complimentary food, drinks, or messages.

In many structured service environments, staff are limited by formal structures in what they can and cannot do and, by this, how they can assist a guest. Comments that can typically be associated with reviews of delighted guests include:

- The staff did not say no at any time.
- The staff were so warm and friendly, and nothing was too much.

- The staff continuously made extra efforts to accommodate us.
- The staff gave us excellent tourist recommendations.
- The staff were so helpful in organizing tours/transport.

The rich context often found in online guest reviews gives a good insight into how this typically works. The guest has a problem or need and knows rationally that it cannot reasonably be expected from the hotel staff to fulfill this need. In small-scale, personalized settings, however, the host can pick up on this and is able to facilitate this need with a solution that is not impeded by limits of the job description, a workload that does not allow to spend too much time on any one guest, or hotel procedures that do not allow to move outside of established protocols.

Even the wealthiest of guests appreciate an upgrade or a discount. It makes one feel acknowledged and cared for. We are not talking about loyalty schemes that entitle the frequent traveler to certain perks, but the ad hoc acknowledgment of a guest's unique situation that is celebrated or rewarded. Also, the service recovery paradox[3] fits in this category. It refers to the idea that when a guest has a negative experience, but the hotel goes above and beyond to correct the issue and provide excellent service recovery, the guest may end up even more satisfied than they would have been if the problem had not occurred. Also here, small independent hotels seem to have a competitive advantage in being able to swiftly, and with full consideration of the individual guests' needs, remedy the situation through a discount or an upgrade.

Hotel guests also love to come into their room to find a present, food, drinks, or a message that they know is left specifically for them. As much as a standard chocolate on the pillow may be appreciated, guests know what is a "hotel standard" and what is genuine care and attention.

A personalized food presentation would look like this:

A guest raves at breakfast about how much he loves the fresh pineapple that is being served. Later in the afternoon, after having
gone out, this same guest finds a small plate with fresh pineapple
in his room with a note from the chef that he found some extra
pineapple and thought the guest would appreciate some more.

The ability to catch on to small things like this tends to be possible
only in small service settings where guests and hosts have a more personal
interaction and the host has more leeway to be creative.

Takeaways

What can we learn from this? First, we have to let go of the notion that the epitome of service excellence can be achieved in large, highly structured, and standardized organizations. If one seeks to delight consumers, one has to perhaps trade size, efficiency, and structure for a more intimate service setting where employees are empowered to deliver truly personalized services.

This observation is really not that surprising when it is unpacked. Our highest need as consumers is perhaps to be recognized and have our unique personal needs met as we purchase a product or service. Real delight only happens when service becomes really personal and we need a smaller and more intimate setting for this to happen. There are, however, a number of takeaways which apply to hotels at large but transfer easily to other commercial settings:

- When your reviews are not as good as you would want, don't hire a social media or online reputation manager. Rather, invest in your service operations. Excellent operations require very little marketing whereas poor operations cannot be saved by all the marketing in the world.
- Well-trained and empowered staff who can empathize with consumers are critical. Recognize those employees and give them the space to work their magic. Employees should be invited to think on their feet to personalize services, solve guest problems, and show attentiveness beyond the set protocols.

- Creativity typically only happens when the working culture is accommodating to this. Many organizations act mainly on bad reviews and move on quickly past the great ones. More discussions need to take place when delight is created to learn how this was achieved and how it can be done again.
- Efficiency and service excellence do not easily coexist. As Stephen Covey put it aptly: "You can't be efficient with People." If you are really pursuing the highest possible online ratings, prioritize personalized service over efficiency and protocol and give staff the space to give expression to their role of hosts fully.

David defeating Goliath is a story that makes us pay attention when it is told. It not only intrigues us, but teaches us that the status quo can be challenged and redefines how we see things. The bigger opponent doesn't always win. Standardization is not service excellence. And, perhaps, most importantly, the humble David has a fighting chance.

CHAPTER 2

The Foundations

Service Excellence and Consumer Engagement

The way people share their opinions and experiences about products and services has evolved significantly over time. This chapter takes a look at the key milestones in the history of reviews, from the early days of word of mouth (WOM) to the dynamic world of digital reviews and beyond.

From WOM to EWOM

It will have become apparent from the previous chapter that online reviews have changed our marketing landscape dramatically. Online review platforms have given consumers a voice to collaboratively share their experiences and make more informed decisions in less time by learning from the experiences of others. We have to accept that this voice is more powerful than ever before in history and, as a consequence, the consumer has become more powerful than ever before. This chapter explores the concept of online reviews, what types we can identify, and how they relate to online reputation management (ORM) efforts.

The history of customer feedback can be traced back to the age-old practice of WOM communication. As societies evolved, so did the ways in which people shared their opinions and experiences. This section will explore the transition from WOM to written reviews and the factors that contributed to this shift.

Before the advent of modern technology, people relied on face-to-face communication to share their experiences and opinions about products and services. WOM recommendations played a crucial role in shaping consumer behavior and influencing the success of businesses. As societies became more literate, written forms of communication, such as letters and newspapers, emerged as additional channels for sharing customer feedback. People started sharing their experiences through letters to friends and family or even letters to the editor in newspapers, which reached a broader audience. With the growth of the publishing industry, consumer magazines began to appear, providing readers with reviews and comparisons of products and services. Expert reviewers and journalists started to play a more significant role in influencing opinions and preferences.

The advent of the Internet brought about a new era of communication, making it easier for people to share their experiences and opinions with a global audience. Online forums, discussion boards, and early review websites provided platforms for consumers to exchange information and feedback on a wide range of products and services. Social media platforms like Facebook, Twitter, and Instagram have revolutionized the way people communicate and share information. Consumers could now post reviews, recommendations, and experiences on their social media profiles, making this feedback accessible to their network of friends and followers. This has led to two radical changes in WOM feedback: amplified reach and access to information.

Amplified Reach

Unlike traditional WOM communication, online reviews can reach a much larger audience. A single review posted on a popular platform can potentially be seen by thousands of people, significantly amplifying its impact on consumer behavior and business reputation.

Accessibility of Information

The Internet has democratized access to information, making it easier for consumers to research products and services before making a purchase. Online reviews provide valuable insights from real users, helping consumers make more informed decisions and reducing the risk of disappointment.

Before online reviews were available, it was already established that dissatisfied customers were more likely to spread negative WOM than satisfied customers were to share positive WOM. Dissatisfied customers

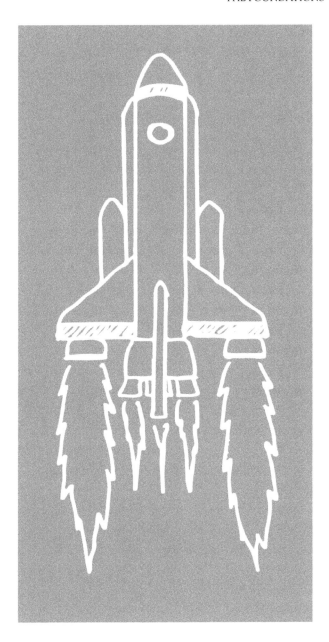

would typically communicate their experience to 7 to 10 people, while satisfied customers would typically share this with two to three people[1].

Although there is no conclusive data on the average reach of online reviews on different platforms, it is safe to say that online reviews are read by hundreds, thousands, or even millions of potential consumers as they orient toward the purchase of a product or service. It is therefore that electronic word of mouth (EWOM) is often referred to as "WOM on Steroids," "WOM on Fire," or "WOM on Steroids With Wings."

Types of Online Reviews

We can distinguish six different types of reviews based on who writes the review and what is being reviewed:

1. **Product Reviews**

   Customers provide feedback on specific products they have purchased or used. These reviews can offer insights into product quality, functionality, durability, and overall customer satisfaction. Product reviews are commonly found on e-commerce platforms, brand websites, and third-party review sites such as Google My Business, eKomi, Yelp, and Amazon.com.

2. **Service Reviews**

   Service reviews focus on customer experiences with services provided by businesses, such as hospitality, transportation, or professional services. These reviews can provide insights into service quality, timeliness, customer support, and overall satisfaction. They can be found on specialized review platforms, social media, or general review websites such as TripAdvisor, Booking.com, and Trustpilot.

3. **Business Reviews**

   These reviews evaluate the overall performance and reputation of a business, including factors such as customer service, pricing, and product quality. Business reviews can be found on review platforms such as Booking.com, Yelp, and eKomi, as well as social media and other online forums.

4. **Employee Reviews**

   Employee reviews offer insights into the experiences of employees working for a particular company, covering aspects such as company culture, work environment, management, and career growth opportunities. Platforms such as the Glassdoor and Indeed are popular sources for employee reviews.

5. **Expert Reviews**

   Expert reviews are written by professionals or industry experts who evaluate products or services based on their knowledge and experience. These reviews often provide in-depth analysis and can be found on specialized websites, blogs, or magazines such as CNET, Techradar, and Lonely Planet.

6. **Influencer Reviews**

   Social media has also given rise to a new breed of opinion leaders known as influencers. These individuals have amassed large followings on social media platforms and have the power to shape consumer behavior through their recommendations and reviews. Influencer reviews can significantly impact the perception of a product or service, either positively or negatively. In addition to prominent influencers with large followings, micro-influencers—those with a smaller but highly engaged audience—have also gained prominence. Brands often collaborate with micro-influencers to tap into niche markets and foster authentic connections with their target audience. Influencer reviews and social media recommendations have become a significant factor in the consumer decision-making process. Consumers often turn to influencers and their social media networks for product recommendations, which can influence their purchasing decisions and brand perceptions.

Service Excellence as a Prerequisite

While companies cannot control directly what their customers write in online reviews, they can manage online reviews to some extent. However, prior to managing online reviews, which typically happens after the product or service is rendered, one would like to optimize one's chances of getting as many positive reviews as possible. It is clear from the earlier points made in this chapter and in Chapter 1 that companies whose customers rave about them have a very easy job in managing their online reputation whereas those who are scolded by the bulk of their customers cannot compensate for this with all the marketing in the world.

A starting point for successful online review marketing is therefore to ensure that the basis of this marketing, that is, the reviews, are overwhelmingly positive. This is done through service excellence. Service excellence can be defined as:

The ability of a business or organization to consistently exceed customer expectations while fostering positive relationships with them.[2]

Service excellence goes beyond simply meeting the basic needs or expectations of customers. Instead, it involves delivering exceptional service that delights customers and creates positive experiences, leading to customer loyalty and advocacy. However, most definitions on service excellence also clearly stipulate the need for fostering positive relationships with one's customers. These relationships need to be based on trust, transparency, and clear communication.

To achieve service excellence, businesses need to prioritize customer satisfaction and establish a culture of continuous learning and improvement. This involves training employees to provide exceptional service, empowering them to solve problems and make decisions, and using feedback and metrics to continuously learn how service delivery can be further improved.

A special mention needs to be made on employee relations or human resrouce management (HRM). The first researchers who explored service excellence in the 1980s identified that well-trained, motivated, facilitated, empowered, challenged, and happy employees lay at the foundation of successful service delivery. In 1994, Heskett and colleagues took this notion further when they introduced "The Service-Profit Chain,"

which introduced the concept and presented empirical evidence to support its validity[3].

The service-profit chain presents four interlinked concepts of service business success:

Internal service quality: The first component is providing a quality service to internal employees. Internal service quality creates satisfied, more effective, and motivated employees who can create better customer opportunities.

Employee satisfaction: Satisfied employees who feel they are being treated well tend to provide quality customer service. Thus, it produces happy customers that lead to customer loyalty.

Customer loyalty: Loyal customers keep coming back, resulting in repeat business as well as positive WOM.

Financial performance: Financial performance is the result of loyal repeat customers and a positive WOM driving revenues and profits over time.

Although the service-profit chain idea was introduced nearly 30 years ago, it remains true today: customer loyalty is driven by employee satisfaction which is driven by internal quality. All lie at the foundation of positive online reviews.

Online Reputation Management or Online Review Marketing?

The common term for the practice of trying to maximize one's online image is ORM. It is typically defined as *the practice of monitoring and influencing the online reputation of a person, brand, or organization*[4]. It involves monitoring online reviews, social media, and search engine results to ensure that positive information appears about the individual or business when people search for them online. The goal of ORM is to create a positive online reputation, manage negative reviews or feedback, and minimize the impact of any negative information on the brand or individual. A limiting factor of ORM's definition and focus is perhaps that it implies that one can indeed *manage* one's own reputation regardless of what happens with consumers who purchase goods and services from the company.

Online review marketing has a different focus as it refers to *the practice of placing online reviews at the center of one's marketing research, considerations, and actions.* As much as it is similar to ORM, they are not the same in that ORM believes, sometimes falsely, that it can control the online reputation whereas online review management starts with the premise that as much as it can highlight and use reviews, it cannot oppose, replace, or influence them directly. The goal of online review marketing is therefore to use authentic and real consumer review data to learn from to optimize one's products and service provision, analyze competitors, identify best practices, define marketing communication, and set pricing strategies. It also acknowledges that online reviews are primarily managed through internal quality leading to service excellence, as opposed to responses that are made after the service was delivered. In that context, one could look at online review marketing as a proactive version of ORM.

The Online Review Marketing Pyramid

The view that online reviews from customers are critical for any of the other reputation management or marketing activities to be effective can be visualized with a pyramid-shaped model.

Similar to Maslow's pyramid of the hierarchy of needs[5], successful online review marketing requires a foundation of an internal quality culture that drives service excellence, similar to Maslow's physiological and safety needs requiring to be fulfilled before the higher needs can be addressed. Service excellence, in turn, drives positive online reviews which are a prerequisite for any effective marketing or reputation management activities to commence. This is outlined in Figure 2.1, the online review marketing pyramid.

Figure 2.1 The online review marketing pyramid

Case Study: Visit Group

Shaping Experiences Through Feedback: ESS Group's
Guest-Centric Approach

ESS Group is a European hospitality organization with a diverse portfolio
of unique hospitality businesses in Sweden, Denmark, and Norway. Their
focus on quality-driven operations aims to create memorable moments
across diverse destinations.

Key performance indicator (KPIs) such as net promoter score (NPS[*6])
and employee net promoter score (eNPS) are their leading indicators

---

[*] NPS measures the loyalty of customers to a company based on one simple question: "How likely is it that you would recommend our company/product/service
to a friend or colleague on a scale of 1-10?" These scores are then categorized as

toward profitability and they are very explicit in their commitment to transparent and authentic communication with their customers:

We are always honest in our communication to our guests, both digitally and in person. The experiences we communicate create expectations that we want to exceed during every single stay. By thinking and acting long term in everything we do, we create regulars, ambassadors, and relationships.

ESS Group is innovative, bold, and not afraid to try new things. This means that sometimes they get things right and sometimes they don't. To mitigate missing the mark, the group proactively collects ratings and reviews through their own guest survey after every stay or visit. This guest-centric approach ensures valuable feedback is obtained, allowing them to address concerns and remedy these issues fast should they not get it right.

In November 2022, ESS Group proudly unveiled their newest destination. However, by December, they recognized that guest feedback was critical and their NPS fell short; there was an urgent need for improvement. Especially one of the restaurants at the new hotel was criticized. ESS Group took immediate action and used its unique resources by deploying food & beverage (F&B) experts from their other locations, harnessing their collective expertise to uplift the service concept in record time. The online guest feedback was used to guide improvements to the service concept and soon after, the NPS increased as a consequence.

This case teaches us that, first, we can't expect to always get things right immediately, especially if we launch unique and innovative service concepts. It further shows us that through immediate action on the ground and in the operation, a recovery can be made swiftly. ESS did not start a media campaign to address the issue, but deployed its resources to where they were needed: on the ground and inside the operation using its strength as a group with strong expertise in their staff.

---

detractors (score 1-6), passives (7-8), and promoters (9-10). The NPS is then calculated by deducting the percentage of detractors from the percentage of promoters.

CHAPTER 3

Online Review Data Collection

Online marketplaces have become an essential source of review data, as they provide a platform for customers to share their experiences and opinions about products and services. This section will explore the role of online marketplaces in the collection and dissemination of review data and their impact on businesses and consumers.

Major e-commerce platforms like Amazon, eBay, and Alibaba serve as critical sources of customer feedback. These platforms enable customers to post reviews on specific products they have purchased, providing insights into product quality, functionality, and overall satisfaction.

Vertical marketplaces specialize in specific industries or product categories, such as Etsy for handmade goods, ASOS for fashion, or Houzz for home improvement. These platforms also facilitate the exchange of review data, enabling customers to share their experiences and opinions about products and services relevant to the specific niche.

Platforms like Uber, Airbnb, and TaskRabbit focus on providing services rather than selling physical products. These marketplaces also gather and share review data, allowing customers to rate and review their experiences with service providers.

Local business directories, such as Yelp and Google My Business, are another source of review data, as they enable customers to rate and review local businesses. These platforms provide valuable insights into the overall performance and reputation of businesses, covering factors such as customer service, pricing, and product quality.

Many online marketplaces aggregate review data from various sources, providing consumers with a more comprehensive overview of a product or service. Online marketplaces play a vital role in establishing trust and credibility for products and services. High ratings and positive reviews can significantly impact a consumer's decision to purchase, while negative feedback can deter potential customers. Businesses must actively manage their online presence and reviews to maintain a positive reputation and build consumer trust.

Review Aggregation

Review aggregator websites gather customer feedback from multiple sources, such as online marketplaces, social media platforms, and dedicated review websites. By presenting a comprehensive overview of a product or service's ratings and reviews, these websites help consumers make more informed decisions and reduce the risk of purchasing a product or service that doesn't meet their expectations.

Some review aggregator websites focus on specific industries, such as Rotten Tomatoes for movies, Metacritic for video games, Google Reviews for travel industry, or Goodreads for books. These platforms provide consumers with a tailored experience and expert opinions, which can be particularly helpful in niche markets.

Review aggregator websites often include comparison tools that allow consumers to compare products or services based on various factors, such as prices, features, or customer ratings. This can help consumers identify the best option for their needs and make more informed purchasing decisions.

Businesses can use review aggregator websites to monitor their online reputation and gain insights into customer feedback from various sources. By analyzing this data, businesses can identify trends, pinpoint areas for improvement, and make informed decisions to drive growth and success.

These websites can help businesses increase their online visibility by featuring their products or services alongside competitors. A positive reputation on these platforms can improve a business' chances of attracting new customers and retaining existing ones.

While review aggregator websites offer valuable insights for businesses and consumers, they also present challenges and limitations. These include the potential for manipulation through fake reviews, the possibility of outdated or incomplete information, and the varying quality of reviews from different sources.

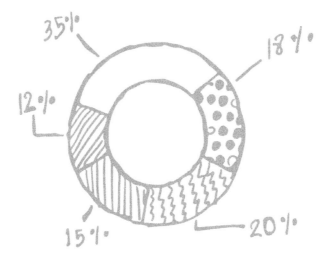

Social Media Platforms

Social media platforms provide users with the tools to create and share their own content, including reviews, recommendations, and testimonials. Social media allows for real-time feedback, enabling customers to share their experiences as they happen. This immediacy can provide businesses with timely insights into their products and services, allowing them to respond quickly to customer concerns and capitalize on positive feedback.

Social media platforms also offer businesses an opportunity to engage directly with their customers, respond to feedback, and demonstrate their commitment to customer satisfaction. This can help businesses build stronger relationships with their customers and foster customer loyalty.

In addition, social media platforms amplify the reach and impact of reviews, as content can quickly spread through shares, likes, and reposts/ retweets. This can have a significant influence on a business's reputation, either positively or negatively, depending on the nature of the feedback.

Social media has also given rise to influencers who can shape consumer behavior through their recommendations and reviews. Influencer reviews on social media platforms can significantly impact the perception of a product or service, either positively or negatively.

Businesses can use social media listening and monitoring tools to track customer feedback and sentiment across various platforms. By analyzing this data, businesses can identify trends, pinpoint areas for improvement, and make informed decisions to drive growth and success. Social media platforms can be powerful tools for reputation management, allowing businesses to address negative feedback, showcase positive reviews, and engage with their customers to maintain a positive online presence. Examples of companies doing this are Obi4wan.com, sproutsocial.com, and hootsuite.com.

Numbers, Text, or Emojis?

Online guest reviews would typically present text, numbers, and sometime emojis. Each has its own unique value to tell us the story of how customers experienced dealing with a service.

Numbers

Guest reviews typically present some sort of numerical data to express satisfaction of the experience. TripAdvisor asks guests to rate elements on a scale of 1 to 5, Booking.com on a scale of 1 to 10, and Amazon asks for 1 to 5 stars. This data provides a very objective measurement that can be analyzed and compared very easily. We can calculate the average score, how consistent this score is over time, how it relates to our competitors, and so on. What numerical ratings do not provide us is context. What is the bigger picture in which this happened, why did it happen, and is this something that we should pay attention to? For context, we need text.

Text

To understand context, we need text. The real value of reviews is that they allow us to step in the shoes of the guest and walk with them through our organization as they engage with us. Reviewers like to share their stories and often give us much more than we asked for. They will outline the "why" of their purchase or visit, they will clarify what they were expecting, and from thereon explain to us what happened and how it made them feel. This context is invaluable in that it gives a real insight into our customers and how we can better serve them.

Text provides us with a story of what happened and how that made the customer feel. It provides us with much more comprehensive information on how our services and processes are experienced. Text thus provides meaning to the numbers and, where text may prove insufficient, we have emojis to enrich it.

Emojis

Emojis became popular due to their ability to add emotional nuance to an otherwise flat text. The initial set of emojis was created by artist Shigetaka Kurita for the mobile platform "i-mode" in Japan in the late 1990s and this proved quite popular. The introduction of an official emoji keyboard to iOS in 2011 and to Android two years later further contributed to their popularity and worldwide use.

Emojis have emerged as a valuable tool for enhancing reviews, offering an expressive means of conveying emotions and sentiments. The visual representation of emotions adds depth and emotional nuance to reviews, enabling companies to better understand customer experiences.

Another advantage is that the intuitive nature of emoji transcends language barriers, enhancing the accessibility of reviews for a global audience, although culturally, some awareness is required. For instance, a thumbs-up emoji is seen as a positive sign of agreement in most western cultures whereas in some parts of the Middle East and Greece, it may be considered an offensive gesture. A hands-together emoji is often used to symbolize prayer whereas in Japan where it originates, it was meant to convey "please" or "thank you."

Besides these cultural challenges, emojis are poised to play an even more significant role in reviews to enrich text with visual sentiment. In addition, emojis allow us to measure satisfaction in a multilingual environment such as an airport of a conference venue.

Data Collection Techniques

There are a multitude of data collection techniques available to obtain data from the customers. In this section, we describe web scraping, the use of application programming interfaces (APIs), survey and feedback forms, and the use of third-party data providers as the most common techniques to obtain this data.

Web Scraping

Web scraping is a popular technique for collecting review data from websites and online platforms. This process involves extracting data from web pages and converting it into a structured format that can be used for analysis. In this section, we will cover the basics of web scraping, discuss tools and libraries, and provide tips for handling common challenges.

> *Understanding web scraping*: Web scraping involves sending HTTP requests to target websites, downloading the HTML content of the pages, and then parsing the content to extract the desired

data. This technique can be applied to collect review data, such as ratings, written reviews, and other relevant information, from various online sources.

Tools and libraries: There are several tools and libraries available for web scraping, depending on your programming language of choice. Some popular options include Beautiful Soup and Scrapy for Python, Jsoup and HtmlUnit for Java, and Cheerio for Node. js. These libraries help simplify the process of downloading and parsing web pages, allowing you to focus on extracting the necessary data.

Inspecting web pages: To effectively scrape review data, it is essential to understand the structure of the target web pages. By using your web browser's developer tools, you can inspect the HTML source code and identify the relevant elements and their attributes, such as class names or IDs, that will be used for data extraction.

Handling dynamic content: Some websites use JavaScript to load content dynamically, which can pose challenges for web scraping. To handle dynamic content, you may need to use tools like Selenium or Puppeteer, which can interact with web pages as a browser would, allowing you to access and extract content that is loaded via JavaScript.

Pagination and navigation: When collecting review data, you may need to navigate through multiple pages or sections of a website. It is essential to identify the appropriate URL patterns or navigation elements, such as "next page" buttons, and include them in your scraping process to ensure comprehensive data collection.

Rate limiting and respectful scraping: Web scraping can put a strain on a website's server, and some sites may enforce rate limiting to prevent excessive requests. To be a responsible web scraper, adhere to the site's robots.txt file guidelines, implement delays between requests, and avoid scraping during peak traffic hours.

Legal and ethical considerations: Always consider the legal and ethical implications of web scraping. Respect website terms of service, privacy policies, and copyright laws. Ensure that the data collected is used responsibly and complies with applicable data protection regulations.

By understanding the basics of web scraping and using the appropriate tools and libraries, businesses can efficiently collect review data from various online sources. However, it is crucial to be aware of the challenges and limitations of web scraping, such as handling dynamic content and respecting website policies, to ensure responsible and effective data collection.

APIs

Application programming interfaces (APIs) offer a more structured and efficient method for collecting review data from various platforms, such as online marketplaces and social media sites. In this section, we explain the fundamentals of APIs, how to access them, and best practices for managing API rate limits and authentication.

APIs are interfaces that allow different software applications to communicate and share data with each other. They provide a standardized way for developers to access and interact with data from external sources.

APIs can be used to collect review data from various platforms in a more structured and reliable manner compared to web scraping.

To access an API, you typically need to register for an API key or token, which is used to authenticate your requests. This key or token should be included in the HTTP request headers when making requests to the API. Many platforms provide detailed API documentation that outlines the available endpoints, request parameters, and response formats, which can help guide you in collecting the desired review data.

APIs may also require different levels of authentication and authorization, depending on the type of data being accessed. Some APIs may use basic API keys or tokens for authentication, while others may require more advanced methods, such as OAuth, to grant access to specific user accounts or protected resources. When working with APIs, you may encounter errors or exceptions, such as invalid request parameters, rate limit violations, or server errors. It is essential to handle these errors gracefully, implementing error handling and retry mechanisms to ensure your data collection process is robust and reliable.

API responses are typically formatted in JSON or XML, which need to be parsed and converted into a structured format for further analysis or storage. It is important to understand the structure of the API response and extract the relevant review data, such as ratings, written reviews, and other pertinent information.

Surveys and Feedback

Surveys and feedback forms provide businesses with a direct and controlled method of collecting review data from customers. In this section, we cover the design and implementation of effective surveys and feedback forms as well as the importance of ensuring customer privacy and consent.

Survey design: The design of your survey or feedback form is crucial to collecting meaningful review data. Consider the following factors when designing your survey:

a. Purpose: Clearly define the purpose and goals of your survey to ensure that the questions asked will yield actionable insights.

b. Question types: Use a mix of question types, such as open ended, multiple choice, and rating scales, to collect a variety of data.

c. Length: Keep your survey concise and focused to reduce respondent fatigue and improve completion rates.

d. Clarity: Ensure your questions are clear, concise, and unbiased to avoid confusion or biased responses.

Distribution channels: Choose the appropriate channels to distribute your surveys and feedback forms, such as e-mail, QR codes, Wi-Fi, in-app notifications, or even printed forms in physical locations. Selecting the right distribution channel can help increase response rates and ensure that you reach your target audience.

Timing: The timing of your survey is essential to maximize response rates and collect accurate review data. Consider sending your survey or feedback form shortly after a customer interaction, such as a purchase or service experience, while the experience is still fresh in their minds.

Incentives: Offering incentives, such as discounts or entry into a prize draw, can encourage customers to complete your survey or feedback form. However, ensure that the incentives do not bias the responses or lead to dishonest feedback.

Privacy and consent: Respect customer privacy by clearly stating how the collected data will be used and stored, and obtain explicit consent from respondents before collecting their personal information.

Ensure compliance with data protection regulations, such as the General Data Protection Regulation (GDPR) or the California Consumer Privacy Act (CCPA) or the Technology (IT) Act of 2000 in India.

Analyzing and acting on feedback: Once you have collected the review data, analyze the responses to identify trends, patterns, and areas for improvement. Use these insights to inform your business strategies, improve products or services, and address customer concerns.

Follow-up and communication: Demonstrate your commitment to customer satisfaction by following up on feedback and communicating any changes or improvements made based on the collected review data. This can help build trust and loyalty with your customers.

Third-Party Data Providers

In some cases, businesses may choose to acquire review data from third-party data providers. These providers collect, aggregate, and organize review data from various sources, such as online marketplaces, review websites, and social media platforms. In this section, we discuss the benefits and drawbacks of using third-party data providers and considerations for selecting a reliable and reputable provider.

Benefits of Third-Party Data Providers

- *Time and resource savings*: Acquiring review data from third-party providers can save businesses time and resources by eliminating the need to develop and maintain custom data collection processes.
- *Data quality and standardization*: Third-party data providers often have established processes for ensuring data quality and consistency, providing businesses with clean, structured, and standardized review data.
- *Comprehensive coverage*: Data providers may offer access to a broader range of review data from multiple sources, giving businesses a more comprehensive view of customer feedback.

- Expertise and support: Reputable data providers can offer expert advice and support to help businesses make the most of their review data, providing valuable insights and recommendations.

Drawbacks of Third-Party Data Providers

- *Data ownership and control*: When relying on third-party data providers, businesses may have limited control over the data collection process and may not own the collected data outright.
- *Data security and privacy*: Working with third-party data providers can introduce potential security and privacy risks, as businesses must trust that the provider is handling customer data responsibly and in compliance with data protection regulations.

When choosing a third-party data provider, consider the following factors:

- *Reputation and reliability*: Look for providers with a proven track record and positive customer reviews to ensure you receive high-quality data and reliable service.
- *Data coverage and quality*: Assess the provider's data coverage, including the sources and types of review data they offer as well as their processes for ensuring data quality and standardization.
- *Pricing and flexibility*: Compare pricing plans and contract terms to ensure the provider's offerings align with your budget and needs.
- *Data security and compliance*: Evaluate the provider's data security measures and compliance with relevant data protection regulations to ensure your customer data is handled responsibly. Make sure you have a Data Processing Agreement that is compliant with the data protection regulations.
- *Support and expertise*: Consider the level of support and expertise the provider offers, such as data analysis, reporting, and recommendations.

Data Storage

Once review data is collected, it is essential to store and organize the data effectively to facilitate efficient analysis and reporting. This section covers best practices for data storage, including the use of databases, file formats, and data management systems. We also discuss the importance of data security and compliance with data protection regulations.

- *Databases*: Databases are a popular choice for storing review data, as they provide structured storage and efficient querying capabilities. Consider using a relational database, such as MySQL or PostgreSQL, for structured data, or a NoSQL database, like MongoDB or Elasticsearch, for more flexible data storage. When selecting a database, consider factors such as scalability, performance, and compatibility with your data analysis tools.
- *File formats*: Depending on the nature and size of your review data, you might choose to store it in various file formats, such as CSV, JSON, or XML. Select a file format that is both easy to read and write and compatible with your data analysis tools.
- *Data management systems*: Implementing a data management system can help you store, organize, and track review data more effectively. These systems can range from simple file-based storage solutions to more sophisticated data lakes or data warehouses, which can store vast amounts of data from multiple sources and enable advanced analytics and reporting capabilities.
- *Data security*: Ensure that your review data is stored securely to protect sensitive customer information and comply with data protection regulations such as the GDPR or the CCPA. Implement encryption, access controls, and regular backups to safeguard your data from unauthorized access or loss. Ensure that you have the necessary consent from customers, store data securely, and implement processes to handle data subject requests, such as the right to access, rectify, or delete personal data.

- *Data organization and categorization*: Organize your review data by categorizing it into relevant dimensions, such as product or service categories, customer demographics, or time periods. This categorization can help facilitate more efficient data analysis and enable more granular insights into customer feedback trends.
- *Data quality and consistency*: Maintaining data quality and consistency is essential for accurate and reliable analysis.
- Implement data validation and cleaning processes to ensure that your review data is accurate, complete, and consistent.

By storing and organizing review data effectively, businesses can facilitate efficient analysis and reporting, enabling them to gain valuable insights and make data-driven decisions. Implementing robust data security measures and complying with data protection regulations are essential to safeguard customer data and maintain customer trust.

Data Cleaning and Preprocessing

Data cleaning and preprocessing are essential steps in preparing review data for analysis. There are various techniques and best practices for handling missing data, removing duplicates, and transforming data to ensure quality and consistency.

Missing data can occur when certain fields or values are not provided by the review source or when errors occur during data collection.

To handle missing data, consider the following techniques:

a. *Deletion*: Remove records with missing data if they represent a small proportion of the dataset and their removal does not introduce bias.

b. *Imputation*: Estimate missing values based on other available data, such as using the mean, median, or mode of the available values, or employing more advanced techniques like regression or machine learning models.

c. *Flagging*: Create a separate indicator variable to identify records with missing data, allowing for separate analysis or handling of these records.

Duplicate records can occur due to data entry errors, data merging issues, or other inconsistencies. Identify and remove duplicate records to ensure data accuracy and prevent overrepresentation of certain data points in your analysis.

Review data often includes unstructured text data, such as written reviews or comments. Perform text cleaning to remove unwanted characters, correct spelling errors, and standardize capitalization, spacing, and punctuation. This process can help improve the quality of the text data and facilitate more accurate text analysis. Transform your data to ensure consistency and enable more effective analysis.

Common data transformations include:

a. *Standardization*: Convert variables to a common scale or format, such as converting all ratings to a consistent scale or standardizing date formats.

   b. *Normalization*: Rescale variables to a standard range, such as between 0 and 10, to facilitate comparison and analysis.

   c. *Discretization*: Convert continuous variables into discrete categories or bins, making them easier to analyze and interpret.

   d. *One-hot encoding*: Convert categorical variables into binary variables, allowing for easier analysis with certain machine learning algorithms.

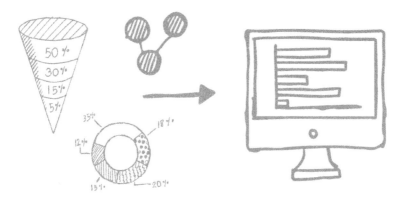

Create new features or variables from the existing data to capture additional information or relationships within the data. For example, you might create a variable representing the length of a written review, the sentiment expressed in the review, or the time since the last review.

Divide your dataset into separate training, validation, and testing sets to ensure unbiased evaluation of your analysis methods and models. This process can help prevent overfitting and improve the generalizability of your findings.

By implementing data cleaning and preprocessing techniques, businesses can improve the quality and consistency of their review data, facilitating more accurate and reliable analysis. These steps are critical to extracting valuable insights from review data and informing data-driven decision making.

Ethical Considerations and Data Privacy

When working with review data, it is crucial to consider ethical implications and adhere to data privacy regulations. Make sure you always respect the privacy of your customers and obtain explicit consent for data collection, inform customers about how their data will be used, and provide options for customers to access, modify, or delete their personal information.

Implement robust security measures to protect customer data from unauthorized access, data breaches, or other security incidents.

Employ encryption, access controls, and regular backups to ensure the safety of your data.

Collect and retain only the data that is necessary for your analysis and business objectives. Avoid collecting excessive or irrelevant information, and regularly review and delete data that is no longer needed.

Use anonymization or pseudonymization techniques, such as data masking or aggregation, to protect the identity of customers in your review data. This can help reduce the risk of privacy violations and ensure compliance with data protection regulations.

Be aware of potential biases in your review data, such as sampling bias or self-selection bias, and take steps to mitigate their impact on your analysis. Employ robust statistical techniques and validate your findings with multiple data sources to ensure the accuracy and reliability of your insights.

Make sure you are transparent about your data collection, analysis, and reporting processes. Provide clear and accessible information about how review data is used and the measures taken to ensure ethical and responsible data handling.

Familiarize yourself with relevant data protection regulations and ensure that your data collection, storage, and analysis processes are compliant. This may involve implementing processes for handling data subject requests, conducting data protection impact assessments, and appointing a data protection officer.

By consistently considering ethical implications and adhering to data privacy regulations, businesses can ensure responsible handling of review data and maintain customer trust. Implementing best practices for data privacy and addressing potential biases in analysis will help businesses extract valuable insights from review data while minimizing risks and potential harm.

Case Study: Qatar Hotel Classification System and Olery.com

Olery.com is a company that provides online reputation management and guest feedback solutions to the hospitality industry. In 2014, Qatar's Ministry of Tourism partnered with Olery.com to develop a new hotel classification system for the country. This system aims to improve the tourism industry by integrating online guest feedback into the hotel rating system.

Olery.com integrates online guest feedback into the hotel classification system via their TES (Traveller Experience Score), a tool developed by Olery.com that aggregates online ratings from a multitude of online review platforms into one percentage that expresses the average online rating score for a hotel. The new hotel classification system requires a minimum TES score for each respective hotel rating category and if this score is not obtained, a hotel may lose its hotel rating. The new classification system also provides a breakdown of the Guest Experience Index into seven key areas: comfort, cleanliness, food and beverage, reception services, location, amenities, and value for money.

Olery.com's technology aggregates guest feedback from online review sources and assigns a score to each hotel, which is then verified and supplemented by trained and certified inspectors who conduct on-site inspections to corroborate the online-based ratings. The inspectors examine various aspects of the hotel, including room and bathroom quality, service, food and beverage, recreation, facilities and amenities, and cleanliness. The final classification rating is issued by Qatar Tourism Authority's Licensing Department.

Further sentiment analysis can provide inspectors with key areas of focus in the different hotels, and TES comparison with competing destinations provides invaluable insight in the competitiveness of Qatar as a destination.

Integrating online feedback into a hotel classification system allows for a more objective and transparent method of evaluating the quality of hotels, reducing the subjectivity and bias of traditional classification systems. By doing so, travelers can make more informed decisions on where to stay, boosting the reputation of hotels that provide outstanding service and quality and improving the overall tourism industry in the region.

Case Study: Trustpilot

Trustpilot is an open, independent, global review platform where any consumer with a genuine experience can review any business for free, without needing to be invited. Any business can also collect reviews and reply to them for free.

"The principle of being 'open to all' is fundamental to everything we do." Trustpilot was created in 2007 with a mission of becoming a universal symbol of trust, connecting businesses with consumers to foster trust and inspire collaboration. That mission is the same today.

In 2022, over 46 million reviews were written on Trustpilot, which amounts to an enormous amount of data and insights that businesses can use to improve their customer service and marketing strategy.

Reviews on Trustpilot provide real-time analytics and insights that are invaluable to businesses, which can also use the platform as a marketing tool.

Customer feedback is an important part of operating a successful business. New trends in reviews could provide insights into challenges customers are facing, providing businesses with an opportunity to take swift action to help minimize lost revenue.

There are many Trustpilot customer case studies that quantify the difference in customer sentiment and keywords commonly used, providing real-time insights that businesses use to improve their processes. Some of the processes that can be improved using this data include:

- Finding the pricing sweet spot
- Effectively managing shipping expectations
- Identifying website issues
- Improving and recognizing your workforce
- Overcoming sizing challenges
- Managing third-party support ticket vendors

- Putting customer service first
- Identifying additional needs from customers

Homerr is an independent network in the Netherlands for the delivery and return of online purchases which has been using Trustpilot as part of its customer service strategy since 2019. Using Trustpilot data, they were able to design and launch a new retail shipping service and enhance their business as a result.

CHAPTER 4

Online Review Data Analysis

Once the review data has been collected and prepared, the next step is to analyze it to uncover valuable insights. This chapter outlines various analysis techniques that can be applied to review data, each offering unique perspectives and insights into customer opinions and experiences.

Sentiment Analysis

Sentiment analysis, also known as *opinion mining*, is a natural language processing (NLP) technique used to determine the sentiment or emotion expressed in a piece of text, such as a product review or social media post. In this section, we discuss the importance of sentiment analysis in review data, the methods used to perform sentiment analysis, and the challenges associated with this technique.

By analyzing the sentiment expressed in reviews, businesses can:

- Identify strengths and weaknesses in their offerings.
- Monitor customer sentiment over time to assess the impact of changes or improvements.
- Detect emerging trends or issues and respond proactively.
- Compare customer sentiment across different products, services, or competitors.

The use of AI provides many more opportunities for sentiment analysis. We explore these possibilities in Chapter 6.

Topic Modeling

Topic modeling is an unsupervised machine learning technique used to discover underlying themes or topics within written comments. In this section, we discuss the importance of topic modeling for review data, the methods used to perform topic modeling, and the challenges associated with this technique.

Topic modeling provides the following advantages:

- Identify common customer concerns, preferences, or issues.
- Understand customer feedback in a more granular and structured way.
- Discover emerging trends or patterns in customer opinions.
- Segment customers based on their interests or preferences.

Some of the most common techniques include:

a. *Latent Dirichlet allocation (LDA)*: LDA is a generative probabilistic model that assumes each document in a collection is a mixture of a small number of topics, and each word in a document is attributable to one of the document's topics. LDA is widely used for topic modeling due to its simplicity and effectiveness.

b. *Non-negative matrix factorization (NMF)*: NMF is a linear algebraic technique that decomposes a non-negative document-term matrix into two lower-dimensional non-negative matrixes, representing the topics and their distribution across documents. NMF can produce interpretable and meaningful topics, making it a popular choice for topic modeling.

c. *Latent semantic analysis (LSA)*: LSA, also known as latent semantic indexing (LSI), is a dimensionality reduction technique that applies singular value decomposition (SVD) to a document-term matrix, producing a lower-dimensional representation of the documents and terms. This lower-dimensional space can be used to identify latent topics within the dataset.

Some common challenges include:

- *Determining the optimal number of topics*: Selecting the appropriate number of topics for a dataset can be difficult, as it depends on the specific data and objectives of the analysis. Various techniques, such as coherence scores or model perplexity, can help guide this decision.
- *Interpretability of topics*: The topics generated by topic modeling algorithms may not always be easily interpretable or meaningful. Careful examination of the most representative words for each topic and validation with domain experts may be necessary to ensure the topics are relevant and useful.
- *Preprocessing and feature engineering*: The quality of the input data can significantly impact the performance of topic modeling algorithms. Effective preprocessing techniques, such as tokenization, stop word removal, and stemming or

lemmatization, are crucial for improving the quality and interpretability of the resulting topics.

By performing topic modeling on review data, businesses can uncover underlying themes and trends in customer feedback, enabling them to better understand and address customer needs and concerns. However, it is essential to be aware of the challenges associated with topic modeling and consider these when interpreting the results of your analysis.

Text Classification

Text classification is a machine learning task that involves categorizing texts into different predefined classes or categories based on their content. The goal of text classification is to automatically classify a given text document into one or more categories based on its content.

Text classification is widely used in various applications, such as spam filtering, sentiment analysis, document categorization, news classification, and content recommendation. It is also an essential component of many NLP tasks.

There are various approaches to text classification, including rule-based systems, statistical models, and machine learning algorithms. One of the most popular machine learning algorithms used for text classification is the Naive Bayes algorithm, which is based on Bayes' theorem.

In Naive Bayes, the algorithm builds a probabilistic model for each category based on the training data. When classifying a new text document, the algorithm calculates the probability of the document belonging to each category and selects the category with the highest probability.

Other machine learning algorithms used for text classification include support vector machines (SVMs), decision trees, and neural networks. These algorithms are trained on labeled data, and the quality of the classification model depends on the quality and size of the training dataset.

Text classification can also be performed using pretrained models such as BERT, GPT-3, or other language models, which have shown impressive performance in various NLP tasks. These models are trained on large-scale datasets and can be fine-tuned for specific classification tasks with a relatively small amount of labeled data.

Overall, text classification is a powerful technique that enables machines to automatically categorize and understand the content of text documents. It has numerous applications in various industries and is a key component of many advanced NLP systems.

Review Summarization

Review summarization is the process of condensing a longer review or set of reviews into a shorter, more concise version that captures the main points and opinions expressed by the reviewers. This process can be done manually by reading through each review and identifying the key themes and sentiments, or it can be automated using NLP techniques.

The goal of review summarization is to provide readers with a quick and easy way to understand the overall sentiment and key points of a product or service without having to read through every single review. It can also be useful for businesses to analyze customer feedback and identify areas for improvement. However, it is important to note that automated review summarization can sometimes miss important nuances and context that may be present in the original reviews.

Time Series Analysis

Time series analysis is a statistical technique used to analyze and forecast patterns and trends over time. It is a method of analyzing data points collected at regular intervals over time, such as daily, weekly, monthly, or yearly. Time series analysis is commonly used in fields such as finance, economics, weather forecasting, and sales forecasting.

One of the key components of time series analysis is identifying and modeling the underlying pattern of the data. This can involve identifying trends, seasonality, and cyclic patterns. Once the pattern has been identified, statistical models can be used to forecast future values of the time series.

Common techniques used in time series analysis include autoregressive integrated moving average (ARIMA) models, exponential smoothing, and Fourier analysis. These methods can be used to identify and quantify patterns in the data, as well as to make predictions about future values of the time series.

Overall, time series analysis is a powerful tool for understanding and predicting trends and patterns over time. It can be used in a wide range of fields and applications and can provide valuable insights into the behavior of complex systems.

Review Clustering

Review clustering is an NLP technique used to group together similar reviews based on their content. The goal of review clustering is to identify patterns and themes within a large set of reviews, which can be used to gain insights into customer preferences, opinions, and behaviors.

The process of review clustering involves several steps. First, the text of each review is preprocessed, which involves removing stop words, stemming, and identifying important phrases and concepts. Next, a clustering algorithm is applied to group similar reviews together based on the similarity of their content. This can be done using a variety of techniques, such as k-means clustering, hierarchical clustering, or LDA.

Once the reviews have been clustered, the results can be analyzed to identify common themes and sentiments expressed by customers.

This can be useful for businesses to understand what aspects of their products or services are most important to customers, as well as to identify areas for improvement.

However, it is important to note that review clustering is not a perfect technique and may not always produce accurate results. This is because natural language is complex and can contain multiple interpretations, making it difficult to accurately capture the nuances of human expression. Additionally, review clustering may not be effective for smaller datasets or when the reviews are highly diverse in content.

Case Study

MMGY TCI Research Combining Surveys and Big Data for Destination Insights

MMGY TCI Research is a global travel research company that uses a data-driven approach to provide insights to their clients in the travel and tourism industry. TCI Research helps destination management companies (DMO) and travel brands globally navigate the complex and competitive visitor economy through data. They measure performance and identify trends and data-based insights to help brands stand out from the competition. They do so by using standard and custom advanced research solutions based on conventional surveys and curated big data technology integration.

MMGY TCI's TRAVELSAT Competitive Index is a tool that provides a great example on how online review analysis can lead to intelligence on a destination level. It is a ranking system that measures the competitiveness of countries in the tourism industry using online review data. The index is based on a set of criteria, including natural and cultural resources, infrastructure, and services related to the tourism industry. The index is published by the Travel and Tourism Competitiveness Reports, dashboards, and APIs.

The TRAVELSAT Competitive Index aims to provide a comprehensive assessment of the factors that contribute to the competitiveness of countries in the tourism industry. The index is designed to help policymakers, investors, and other stakeholders make informed decisions about where to invest in the tourism industry.

The TRAVELSAT Competitive Index is calculated by analyzing online review and rating data from various sources, such as TripAdvisor, Booking.com, and other travel review websites. TCI Research has developed a proprietary NLP algorithm that processes all these reviews in search of a set of predefined categories and attributes.

The TRAVELSAT Competitive Index is one of the most widely recognized and respected ranking systems in the tourism industry. It is used by governments, tourism organizations, and investors to assess the competitiveness of countries in the tourism industry and to identify opportunities for growth and development.

MMGY TCI's algorithm analyzes online reviews for granular data relating to various aspects of the travel experience, such as attractions, accommodation, dining, transportation, shopping, nightlife, and safety and security. The algorithm assigns a "sentiment score" to each aspect analyzed based on the frequency and tone of the reviews. It then aggregates the scores for each attribute and category to provide an overall competitive index for the destination.

Additionally, MMGY TCI Research compares the sentiment scores obtained from the analysis of online reviews with benchmarked destinations to provide context and identify areas of strengths and weaknesses in the TCI's destination compared to its competitors, proving critical information for destination planning, brand management, industry stakeholder management, and product development.

The TRAVELSAT Competitive Index has become one of the most widely recognized and respected ranking systems in the tourism industry. It is used by governments, tourism organizations, and investors to assess the competitiveness of countries in the tourism industry and to identify opportunities for growth and development (*Source*: www.tci-research.com).

CHAPTER 5

Strategic Marketing Using Online Review Data

This chapter explores strategic marketing opportunities using online review data. When collected, cleaned, and analyzed correctly, online review data provides a wealth of information that gives companies an opportunity to better align their product and service offering to their customers, analyze their competitive advantage, enhance customer engagement, streamline their marketing communication, create unique marketing content, and optimize pricing strategies. This chapter ends with a reflection on how online reviews feed an economy of trust and the need to be authentic, transparent, and honest in online review marketing. However, first, we need to understand what online review data does and does not tell us.

Understanding the Data

The starting point of strategic marketing using online reviews is to understand what the data contains. There are some considerations that should be taken note of:

1. What customers say in their reviews is true to them.
2. What customers say in their reviews is important to them and therefore deserves focus.
3. However, the customer in question may not be your customer. Sometimes, a bad review means that the wrong customer came in and there was no way for you to satisfy them with your product or service.
4. The solution to problems may not lie in your product or service, but in expectation management and other surrounding factors.

The fact that most reviews are accompanied by ratings gives us opportunity to analyze how important something is for the customer that has left a review. Consider this: a customer writes a review on a hotel stay that is positive in sentiment. The review does contain a critical comment that there was a bit of a wait on check-in; however, this is followed by a description of how the receptionist was warm, effective, and extremely helpful. This review is accompanied with a rating of 10 out of 10, also on the subcategories. Let's assume we see this type of trend recurring regularly in our reviews. What does this mean? It may very well mean that the waiting for check-in is not as important as the actual engagement with the receptionist. Where should the hotel then lay its focus on to drive positive reviews—speed at reception (e.g., hire more receptionists or automate part of the check-in process) or ensuring that the hotel hires, trains, and empowers the most hospitable, helpful, and professional receptionists?

Case Study: VisitBrabant

VisitBrabant is the marketing organization of destination Brabant. Visit-Brabant shows what Brabant has to offer for residents and national and international visitors so that entrepreneurs, regions, cities and villages, nature, and culture and events get the attention and the visitors they deserve. To achieve this, VisitBrabant develops B2C campaigns; however, VisitBrabant also focuses on strengthening the marketing power of Brabant leisure entrepreneurs—among other things, by offering practical services and, for example, by sharing knowledge through meetings and master classes.

About five years ago, the rise of reviews was enormous. That is why VisitBrabant organized a master class for Brabant entrepreneurs (attractions and museums, accommodation, and catering) on how to use review sites as a marketing channel. During this session and other engagements with entrepreneurs, they learned that there was little knowledge about review management among leisure entrepreneurs. After all, review sites are a (usually free) marketing channel with a lot of impact on potential guests, and therefore a missed opportunity if "our" Brabant entrepreneurs do not handle this optimally.

To empower their entrepreneurs, VisitBrabant set up a review management knowledge program. It is aimed at increasing knowledge about (and the importance of) review management and at stimulating local entrepreneurs to get started with this subject. For this, they use Olery. com. Together, they developed a dashboard with the review data from more than 600 locations in Brabant, from which tailor-made reports could be sent to partners on a monthly basis.

VisitBrabant already achieved a lot in this area, and they will continue to focus on review management so that entrepreneurs present themselves optimally to the potential guests, through their own channels, through VisitBrabant channels, and through other relevant marketing channels such as review sites.

In 2021, VisitBrabant won three marketing prizes at the Grand Prix Marketing Awards. The first was the silver award in the Non-Profit Category for the *"hier-moet-je-zijn"* campaign. The jury was full of praise for the way in which VisitBrabant connected and activated the leisure sector and leisure entrepreneurs. VisitBrabant was also rewarded with no fewer than two gold awards for specific categories within the campaign.

Aligning Product and Service Concept

By analyzing review data, businesses can identify the features and benefits that customers appreciate most in a product or service or what is lacking. This can be done easily by looking for trends in sentiment analysis or the filtering of keywords and, a bit more advanced, correlating this to ratings given by these customers.

Sentiment analysis or the filtering of keywords can quickly and easily present what products or services guests are missing in your business or which performance indicators delight and which detract.

It is, however, important to realize that what guests say in a review can generally be considered to be important for them. However, as mentioned earlier, if there are negative comments with full scores, the interpretation becomes more complex. Did the guest make an error or is the issue really not that important for them? This is a small but critical detail as resources in organizations are typically limited and eliminating every possible negative comment raised may not be possible. The strategy should therefore be directed at those negative comments that are accompanied with poor scores.

In 2019, we looked at how hotel guests experience the sustainability (shared values) focus in hotels by analyzing over one million reviews collected by Olery.com[1]. We wanted to identify to what extent hotel guests talk about and appreciate the sustainable focus of hotels in terms of environmental sustainability as well as in broader corporate sustainability practices. The findings were rather surprising in that only 1 in 1000 guests found sustainability important enough to mention it in their reviews, but those who did were more satisfied with the hotel in question if they explicitly follow a sustainability agenda. These findings tell us that sustainability initiatives (at the time) were perhaps not as important to as many guests as one would think; however, for those to whom it was important, it affected the overall rating.

Research such as this is relatively easy to conduct especially when it concerns one company or a competitive set of data. Before making major investments in overhauling a service, it is therefore wise to conduct an analysis linking comments to ratings to identify their importance. Reviews seem to have an advantage over surveys, especially those aiming to measure future intention by reducing social desirability bias. Social desirability bias occurs when respondents answer questions in a way they think reflects positively on them, even if it is not entirely truthful, which can affect the reliability of the data. As reviews are written with what is top of mind for the consumer without being directed by questions from, for instance, a survey, one can expect to get a more truthful response.

Case Study: Pacific

Reviews provide us with a goldmine of data that can be leveraged for all sorts of digital marketing applications. At PACIFIC, we primarily use review data to drive better website performance and enhance a brand's discoverability in search.

For example, a travel site wanting to inspire visitors to book a trip to a specific destination or property may lean on the social proof that reviews provide. However, they usually leave the reviews in one specific module or section of the page under the title "Reviews." PACIFIC helps them discover the themes, patterns, and highlights these reviews mention and turn them into content that lives all over the page from simple messaging to complex storytelling.

This extrapolation turned into content helps our clients outrank their competitors in Google Search and outperform industry averages for conversion. It guarantees that the power of reviews is blended in throughout the landing page and customer journey so that visitors are more likely to discover and purchase within the same session.

PACIFIC even takes this process one step further through a platform called Natural Language Generation (NLG). Review data is paired with other datasets to create unique content at scale, often for hundreds or thousands of pages all at once. In the case of travel, this output can take the form of custom travel guides or e-mail newsletters. It can also be used as social posts or even descriptions on category and product pages. The obvious benefit is to enrich each page with more relatable content but it also has been proven to help performance on a large scale.

We've also noticed that review themes and highlights are often predictable for certain hotels, activities, or destinations. PACIFIC surfaces these insights up front in the creative process to identify new content or messaging opportunities. For example, a hotel near the beach will also have reviews mentioning how close the property is to the water. We combine reviews that mention the steps or minutes to walk there and average their time estimates as well as their sentiment. Those values can now be called out in more prominent areas of the page like the headline resulting in more conversions because a visitor saw it was *only a 5 minute walk to the beach.*

Market Positioning

Online review data is critical for effective market positioning. First, it assists you in identifying those market segments that are most attractive to you. Second, it allows you to identify the critical success factors (CSFs) that attract and retain those customers. Third, it allows you to formulate or sharpen your unique selling proposition that talks to those market segments and the CSFs that attract and retain them.

The first point of attention is who seems particularly excited about your product or service? Review data can be used to identify customer segments that are particularly enthusiastic about a product or service, allowing businesses to develop targeted marketing and advertising campaigns that resonate with these customers. For example, if a large percentage of customers mention a particular use case or application for a product, businesses can create messaging and creative that speaks directly to that use case.

Consider that the product or service does not appeal to everyone equally and therefore the aim to make everyone happy is an unrealistic one. It happens in any business that the "wrong" customer engages and, despite the best efforts, one ends up with a dissatisfied customer and a negative review. Fred Reichheld, in his book *The Ultimate Question*, refers to this concept as "bad profits."[2] These profits are considered bad as the short-term advantage (profit) is at the expense of (online) reputation in the long run and attracting these customers should therefore be avoided. Online reviews may very well give insight into how this customer ended up purchasing the product or service under a false expectation and this is invaluable information for the marketing team to adjust their communications to discourage such customers to purchase from you.

Review data can also provide businesses with valuable insights into how they compare to their competitors in terms of product quality, customer experience, and overall customer satisfaction. By analyzing customer feedback about competitors, businesses can identify areas where they may be falling short and prioritize efforts to improve their products or services. However, as one makes this comparison, ensure that it is done on those factors that are critical: *the CSFs* that seem particularly important to your specific market segments. As outlined before, CSFs can be identified by sentiment analysis or filtering by keywords and linking this

data to review ratings. This data can then be used to identify competitive advantages and key selling points that cover those CSFs and those are what you want to focus on in your marketing strategy.

It can help businesses understand their competitors' strengths and weaknesses, providing insights into potential opportunities for differentiation. For example, if a business notices that its competitor is receiving a lot of negative feedback about a particular aspect of their product or service, it may be able to capitalize on this by highlighting their own strengths in that area. An example may be that you have a competitor who simply has a superior product; however, this competitor is charging much more than you are and regularly scores low on "value for money," whereas you do not have this problem. It could be that a CSF is "affordability" of the particular product. By focusing on the ability to continue to undercut this competitor in price, you can achieve an overall better rating score, driving more business volume in your direction despite your product being of lesser quality. By then combining this advantage in your explicit selling proposition, you are able to compete successfully.

Case Study Airbnb Winning Market Share With Targeted Advertising

Here is an example of a company that has successfully won market share through targeted advertising.

Airbnb is a company that has been successful in winning market share through targeted advertising. Airbnb uses data and analytics to target its audience with relevant and personalized ads, such as targeting travelers with ads promoting unique and affordable accommodations that fit their travel preferences and budget. Airbnb also uses location-based targeting to reach users who are planning trips to specific destinations, and retargeting to reach users who have shown interest in booking but have not yet completed a reservation.

In addition to targeted ads, Airbnb has also invested in experiential marketing campaigns that appeal to its audience's interests and values. For example, Airbnb's "Live There" campaign encouraged travelers to "live like a local" by staying in authentic and off-the-beaten-path accommodations, highlighting the unique and memorable experiences that Airbnb can offer compared to traditional hotels.

This campaign helped to differentiate Airbnb from its competitors and attract more younger and more adventurous travelers.

Marketing Communication

Marketing and advertising are perhaps the most valuable applications of review data insights. The information of what guests enjoy about a product or service can almost directly be translated into effective marketing communication. The information can then be used to develop messaging and creatives that emphasize these selling points and speak directly to customer needs and preferences.

By analyzing review data, businesses can gain valuable insights into customer preferences and pain points, which can inform more effective marketing and advertising strategies which hit the nail on the head. If you are looking for a suitable credo for your business or your brand, try a sentiment analysis that identifies comments of the most delighted customers. How do they describe their experience and feelings about their interaction with your business?

Online reviews also present us with insight into our weaknesses and these are equally important for the marketing team to take notice of. The worst one can do is boasting about something you think is great, but which constantly seems to disappoint customers. This will not only invoke negative reviews disputing your brand or product promise, but also result in mockery and jokes that affect your campaign in the negative direction.

If marketing promises are inaccurate, online reviews have a tendency to quickly highlight this and the only correct strategy is to either improve quickly or to stop boasting.

More generally, review data can be used to evaluate the effectiveness of marketing and advertising campaigns by tracking how customers respond to messaging and creative. By monitoring review data before, during, and after a campaign, businesses can measure the impact of their efforts and make data-driven decisions about future campaigns.

Case Study: Enhancing Customer Experience With Personalized Recommendations at Booking.com

Booking.com is a travel company that has been successful in enhancing the customer experience with personalized recommendations. Booking.com uses data and analytics to recommend hotels and accommodations to its customers based on their search history, previous bookings, and preferences.

Booking.com's recommendation system is powered by advanced machine learning algorithms that analyze each customer's search and booking behavior to suggest hotels and accommodations that they are likely to prefer. The system takes into account a variety of factors, such as location, price, amenities, and similar properties that other customers have enjoyed.

Booking.com also uses personalized e-mail campaigns to communicate with customers and make personalized recommendations. For example, if a customer has previously booked a beachfront resort, Booking.com might send them an e-mail with personalized recommendations for other beachfront properties in their preferred destinations.

By providing personalized recommendations, Booking.com has been able to improve customer satisfaction and retention. Customers are more likely to return to Booking.com and make repeat bookings when they feel that the platform understands their preferences and offers relevant recommendations.

Customer Engagement Marketing

Excellent reviews may package your message to attract new customers more effectively than any message your marketing team can come up with. It represents the authentic voice of existing customers and nothing speaks more to potential customers than people like them sharing their experiences.

By identifying common themes in customer feedback, businesses can identify opportunities to improve their customer experience and prioritize efforts to address common issues. Review data can also be used to identify loyal customers who are particularly satisfied with a product or service, allowing businesses to engage with them in more meaningful ways and build brand loyalty.

By analyzing review data, businesses can further identify common themes and issues that customers are experiencing with a product or service. This information can be used to develop more personalized communication with customers, such as targeted e-mail campaigns or personalized responses to customer inquiries.

By monitoring review data, businesses can identify customers who are particularly satisfied with a product or service. These customers can be engaged in more meaningful ways, such as through loyalty programs or through targeted marketing campaigns. Engaging with loyal customers can help to build brand loyalty and increase customer lifetime value. When this engagement is kept online and shared in a public space, these conversations can very well result in a spontaneous marketing campaign that is authentic, cost effective, and very powerful.

However, there is more. What about finding influencers who really love your product and engaging with them? An influencer is, in essence, a customer just like your other customers; however, this particular one has an online following and reach, resulting in their voice having a momentous impact on your product, service, and company reputation. The best influencer–company relations would be those that occur organically and remain authentic. The influencer uses the product or service, loves it, and is not afraid to share it. The company engages and invites the influencer to try other products or services and a relationship is born.

Case Study: The Power of Influencer-Based Marketing at Glossier

A company that effectively uses influencer-based marketing is the cosmetics brand, Glossier. Glossier partners with influencers across various social media platforms, including Instagram, YouTube, and TikTok, to promote their products to their followers.

The influencers demonstrate the use of different Glossier products and share their experiences and opinions about the brand. Glossier's influencer marketing campaigns highlight people's "before and after" experiences using Glossier products, creating a relatable and aspirational touch point for potential customers. Glossier's approach to influencer

marketing relies heavily on using micro-influencers or ordinary consumers with smaller followings but high engagement rates. Glossier leverages social proof by showcasing relatable, everyday people using their products, which bolsters their brand's credibility and authenticity.

By partnering with like-minded, aspirational influencers, using real customer testimonials, and delivering on the brand's promise, Glossier has built a powerful and effective influencer marketing strategy that resonates with its audience and drives sales.

Pricing Strategies

The term "value for money" can frequently be identified while analyzing online reviews. It is a "leveler" whereby the consumer relates the quality or experience to the cost that they have incurred. In principle, one can state that the better the quality, the higher the cost is allowed to be, or, in reverse, the higher the cost, the higher the expectation. The introduction chapter highlighted how research has confirmed that higher online review scores lead to an increased revenue per available room. In other words, more satisfied customers result in higher revenues to hotels.

By analyzing customer feedback about pricing, businesses can identify areas where they may be able to charge more or less for a product, as well as opportunities to bundle or unbundle features to create more value for customers. Review data can also be used to monitor how customers respond to pricing changes and make data-driven decisions about pricing adjustments.

By analyzing review data, businesses can identify the features and benefits that customers value most in a product or service. This information can be used to adjust pricing in ways that reflect the value customers place on different features. It helps how customers perceive the value of a product or service compared to competitors.

This information can be used to adjust pricing to remain competitive in the market. By using review data, you can test different pricing strategies and monitor customer responses. For example, businesses may test different pricing models or price points to see how customers respond, and use this data to adjust pricing accordingly.

Some strategies include:

Premium pricing: Companies with consistently high online review scores can leverage their positive reputation to charge premium prices that reflect the quality and value they offer to customers.

Dynamic pricing: Companies can monitor their online review scores and adjust their pricing strategies based on trends that they pick up on. During peak season or when review scores are high, companies can increase prices, while during low season or when review scores are low, they may decrease prices to stimulate demand.

Value-based pricing: Companies can use their online review data to identify the specific features or attributes that customers value the most and adjust their pricing for those services accordingly while discounting products or services that receive lower scores.

Bundle pricing: Companies can use their online review data to identify which products or services are frequently purchased together and create bundled pricing packages that offer a discounted rate compared to purchasing the items separately. This pricing strategy can incentivize customers to purchase more items at once, increasing revenue per transaction and potentially even their online ratings as guests find more value in the transaction. Also, the other way around, unbundling products or services may achieve similar results.

Subscription model: Companies can use online review data to identify which products or services customers frequently purchase and create a subscription model offering these items at a discounted rate. This pricing strategy can incentivize customers to sign up for a subscription and commit to the brand over the long term, while also providing a steady stream of revenue for the company.

Monitor how customers respond to pricing changes and make data-driven decisions about pricing adjustments. By analyzing customer feedback and monitoring sales data while experimenting actively on identified

trends, businesses can adjust pricing in ways that optimize both revenue and customer satisfaction.

Case Study: How TrevPar World Uses Online Reviews in Total Revenue Management

TrevPar World is a hospitality data analytics company with a diverse portfolio of hotels and hotel groups. The group offers full-service solutions for commercial readiness including total revenue management, channel management, global distribution platform connectivity, central reservations, integrated marketing, and brand development services.

The group's core focus is to optimize property profits by implementing unique strategies that allow owners and operators to track, adjust, and improve all performance metrics of their property and all its outlets, in the short and long terms.

In terms of online review marketing, owner and founder Derek Martin is very clear:

Guest Reviews should form part of your business Strategy. For Hotels this starts with your Online Distribution Strategy and using Online Travel Agencies (OTAs). If you are not on Booking.com or you restrict volume on that channel, where are your reviews coming from? Typically we find that more reviews translate to a better average rating and a better attraction for prospective guests. A starting point therefore is to ensure that you distribute sufficient volume using your main OTAs despite the commission costs involved. Your ranking on OTAs is further determined not just by your average review score, but also the volume, so volume is key.

As part of the revenue management process, a hotel is typically compared to the performance in its competitive set which would comprise 5 to 10 hotels in the same destination. It is clear that aligning value and price is critical to being competitive in that destination as Derek explains:

When we take on a new client, we typically find that their ADR (average daily rate) is too low and can be increased without concerns for review scores by expanding the channels amongst which room nights are sold. From thereon, we push the rate up as we watch specifically the "Value for Money" scores in the guest reviews. The moment we start seeing these scores drop, we have two options: either reduce the rate, or strengthen the service offering. The rates charged within the competitive set moderate which option is more likely to be successful.

Through sentiment analysis and filtering of keywords, they would be able to identify where value for money falls short and sometimes this is easy to fix. For instance, guests find the waiting time at breakfast unacceptable for the rate paid. A simple solution may be an additional host at breakfast to redress the value for money score. Another interesting observation that Derek shares has to do with the customer segmentation. He comments:

> *Typically we find that higher paying customers are more balanced in their feedback and as much as they are critical about value for money, it does not automatically follow that the lower your rate, the more satisfied your guests will be. There is a certain price point with every hotel, where you start attracting the wrong customers who have an*

unrealistic expectation of their hotel stay and this can lead to negative reviews. In that case, increasing your rate may bring you back to your appropriate market segments and not only will your revenues increase, but so will your online review scores.

Derek closes off by reiterating the need for integrating your online review data not just in your pricing strategy but in your business strategy itself:

Your business needs to be very aware of who its guests are and what they consider to be value for money. In terms of distribution channel management, it is therefore critical to not only look at the rate you secure, but also which guest is behind this rate and whether this channel will drive online reviews. A healthy distribution mix is therefore important to ensure online review volume, review scores, and input on your value for money proposition.

For more information on TrevParWorld, visit www.trevparworld.com.

The Economy of Trust

As we review these marketing strategies, there is a recurring theme that drives marketing success in the age of online reviews and that is the concept of authenticity and trust. As consumers have access to information and platforms to carry their voice, authenticity of genuine and transparent promises and engagement becomes paramount with trust being perhaps the highest currency that flows from this.

Online reviews have influenced the "economy of trust" by increasing transparency, empowering customers, providing social proof, enabling direct feedback, enhancing credibility, and making reputation management more important. By paying attention to online reviews and engaging with customers authentically and appropriately, businesses can build and maintain high levels of customer trust, leading to increased customer loyalty and positive electronic word of mouth.

Consumers want to be engaged with and be loyal to a brand. However, this engagement and loyalty are based on the belief that the company really is what it says it is and the values it holds dear. If the consumer learns otherwise, the consequences can be damaging. The concept of fake reviews is something that requires specific consideration. Fake reviews can be written by a competitor or other external party that wishes ill on the company; however, it can also refer to companies trying to manipulate their reviews in a dishonest manner.

Dealing with fake reviews can be a challenging task for any company; however, there are several proven strategies to mitigate their impact on your brand's reputation. First, one wants to regularly monitor review platforms, social media, and other relevant channels to identify potential fake reviews. Suspicious patterns, such as multiple negative reviews originating from the same IP address or a sudden surge in reviews within a short period, are clear indicators. One can check if the reviewer has a history of posting similar reviews, assess the language and content for consistency, and compare it with genuine customer experiences or feedback from operations on whether the incident did really occur. Look for any personal biases or irrelevant information that may indicate a fake review.

When a fake review is identified, respond promptly but professionally. Avoid engaging in arguments or directly accusing the reviewer of being fake. Instead, politely request more information about their experience or offer to resolve any legitimate concerns they may have. Most review platforms provide options to flag and report fake reviews.

Take advantage of these features to report the fake reviews and provide any evidence you have collected. Be sure to follow the platform's guidelines and provide detailed explanations to support your claim. Counterbalance the impact of fake reviews; encourage your genuine customers to leave feedback. Provide convenient channels for them to share their experiences, such as through your website, social media, or e-mail. Positive reviews from real customers are the most effective way to help counteract the effects of fake reviews.

Even if a review is fake, it may contain elements of legitimate concerns. Use these reviews as an opportunity to identify areas for improvement in your business. Address any valid issues raised by fake reviews to enhance your products, services, or customer experience. In some cases, fake reviews may violate local laws or regulations. Consult with legal experts to understand your options for legal recourse, such as filing a complaint or taking legal action against individuals or entities responsible for spreading fake reviews.

Beyond other parties writing fake reviews, it may be tempting for companies to engage with companies or individuals that claim that they can "manage" your reviews for you. The advice is simple: stay away from these companies; the short-term gains will most certainly not weigh up to the reputational damage of betraying the trust of your customers.

The values that a business promotes should be lived by consistently not only by its owners, management, and staff, but also by its influencers. It is obvious that the posting of fake reviews or any action which affects the online review content falsely is potentially disastrous. Even if a company would not get caught, the difference between the artificially enhanced reviews and the experience that real customers have is very likely to produce a counter response of bad reviews and comments resulting in a more negative online reputation in the end. Genuine and authentic online reviews should be at the center of the marketing strategy. By being transparent and engaged with your customers and using their voice to define your marketing strategy, you will set your business up for continued growth and success.

Case Study: Amazon and to the Economy of Trust

Amazon recognizes the inherent value of customer reviews as a rich source of feedback and insights. By encouraging customers to leave reviews, Amazon gains a wealth of information that helps identify strengths and weaknesses in its products. Through advanced data analysis techniques, Amazon can identify recurring themes and issues that customers raise in their reviews. Whether it's product quality, packaging, or other aspects, this analysis provides a comprehensive understanding of customer sentiments.

Armed with the insights from review analysis, Amazon employs a data-driven approach to inform its product improvement strategies. By pinpointing areas of concern, Amazon can focus its resources and efforts on making necessary changes to enhance the overall customer experience. Amazon's commitment to continuous improvement is exemplified by its ability to adapt and iterate its products based on review analysis. By actively listening to customer feedback, Amazon can make timely adjustments to address identified issues and deliver products that align with customer expectations.

Through its proactive review analysis and product improvements, Amazon aims to improve customer satisfaction. By addressing concerns raised in reviews, Amazon ensures that its products meet the needs and expectations of its diverse customer base, fostering loyalty and trust. However, with good reviews driving sales, not all Amazon partners always play by the rules. A good example is the company Cure Encapsulations which got into hot water after "buying" positive reviews from a company Amazonverifiedreviews.com to fabricate reviews and give the product five stars[3]. As part of its settlement with the U.S. Federal Trade Commission, it was forced to pay substantial fines and had to send a letter to all registered customers that its claims on its weight loss product were false. It goes without saying that beyond the legal cost and fines imposed, the company's reputation suffered as well.

Amazon acted as well and sued Amazondverifiedreviews.com which went out of business in 2016. Amazon has further implemented a range of measures to prevent the posting of fake reviews. One such measure is the use of automated systems and human moderators to detect and remove fake reviews. The system uses machine learning algorithms to analyze billions of reviews and detect patterns that indicate suspicious activity. Amazon also provides tools for customers to report suspicious reviews. Customers can use the "Report Abuse" feature to flag reviews that they suspect are fake or biased, and Amazon's moderators will investigate the issue and take appropriate action.

In addition to these measures, Amazon has implemented strict policies that regulate the posting of reviews. For example, reviews must be based on personal experience, and sellers are prohibited from offering incentives in exchange for positive reviews. Amazon's position on fake reviews is clear: they do not tolerate them[4]. Amazon understands that the trust of its customers is essential to its success. This customer-centric approach has not only propelled Amazon's growth but also cemented its reputation as a trusted brand. As businesses strive to enhance their products and build strong relationships with customers, harnessing the power of customer reviews, like Amazon does, can serve as a vital tool for success in the economy of trust.

Case Study: Convious

> Convious is the leading e-commerce solution for venues in the attraction visitor industry and delivers a digital customer experience for more than 150 attractions, museums, and theme parks in 14 countries.

Today, there are countless travel and booking sites that encourage visitors to write reviews and every day, hundreds of thousands of reviews get published. However, effective reputation management is more than crunching through thousands of reviews. Therefore, Convious introduced an online reputation module, which is based on technology provided by Olery.com.

This module enables Convious users to automatically collect reviews and analyze them using the latest AI technology. They can detect sentiments on essential topics like pricing, queuing, staff friendliness, and much more. Major steps in the development of AI technology will make reputation management an ever greater part of running a successful business.

The impact of this new technology can be clearly seen at the MOCO (Modern Contemporary) Museum. This Amsterdam-based museum has received over 2.5 million visitors since it opened its doors in 2016. It was spending huge amounts of time every week collecting and analyzing online reviews. After implementing the Reputation Management module, they reduced this to a few hours per week. This was done by collecting reviews automatically, as well as analyzing them on predefined sentiments using AI-powered technology.

Today, with the click of a button, they can accumulate and organize Internet-wide reviews and see which areas of the business customers are rating, from parking to queuing, staffing, and site access. It really has been a game changer for the business because they now have full visibility of customer satisfaction and can manage their expectations.

Convious sees more and more attractions use this technology to collect and closely monitor sentiment in online reviews, which goes hand in hand with the fact that attractions will push for more reviews, making it easier to leave a review.

That reviews are already an integral part of the guest journey is even more relevant. Adding reviews to a platform where you can directly book your tickets will keep the visitor on the same platform and shorten the time from research to actual booking, making an impeccable reputation even more important.

For more information on Convious, visit: www.convious.com.

CHAPTER 6

The Power of AI in Review Data

Artificial intelligence (AI) has emerged as a transformative force across multiple industries, showcasing its remarkable capabilities in the analysis of review data. In an era of rapid online platform and social media expansion, the sheer volume of daily reviews has reached unprecedented levels. This offers a wealth of valuable insights in consumer sentiment. This chapter explores the ways AI harnesses the power of review data, extracting meaningful information, enhancing decision-making processes, and elevating customer experiences.

Sentiment Analysis

One of the key capabilities of AI in review data analysis is automated sentiment analysis. Traditional methods required humans to manually read through each review and categorize the sentiment expressed. However, with AI, algorithms can be trained to analyze text data and determine the sentiment, whether it is positive, negative, or neutral. This process is done at scale, enabling businesses to process large volumes of reviews quickly and efficiently. By automatically categorizing sentiments, AI provides a high-level overview of customer opinions, allowing businesses to identify trends and patterns that can inform strategic decisions.

Let's consider a company in the hospitality industry, specifically a hotel chain. AI can be employed to analyze customer feedback from various sources, such as online reviews, social media comments, and survey responses. It would then run through a three-step process:

1. *Data collection*: The AI system collects customer feedback data from different platforms, including review websites (e.g., TripAdvisor and Yelp), social media platforms (e.g., Twitter and Facebook), and customer satisfaction surveys.

2. *Text preprocessing*: The AI system preprocesses the textual data by removing irrelevant information, such as stop words and punctuation. It also applies techniques like tokenization and stemming to standardize the text.

3. *Sentiment analysis*: Using natural language processing techniques, the AI system performs sentiment analysis on the preprocessed data. Sentiment analysis determines the polarity of customer sentiment expressed in the text, typically categorizing it as positive, negative, or neutral. This analysis can be done at a sentence or document level, depending on the desired granularity.

Identifying Critical Success Factors

AI's prowess in review data analysis extends beyond sentiment analysis, empowering businesses to extract topics and keywords from textual data. By training AI models to identify and categorize various themes discussed in reviews, organizations can gain deeper insights into customer preferences, pain points, and emerging trends. Through analysis of keyword frequency and contextual usage, AI algorithms unveil valuable information about product features, service quality, and customer satisfaction levels. The sentiment analysis is then extended with two further steps:

1. *Identifying critical success factors (CSFs)*: By combining sentiment analysis results with customer satisfaction ratings or other relevant metrics, the AI system identifies CSFs. It identifies the factors that have the most significant impact on customer satisfaction, loyalty, and overall sentiment.

2. *Evaluation and recommendation*: The AI system is then able to present the identified CSFs, ranked by importance and associated sentiment. This information can be used to evaluate the performance of the service organization against these CSFs. The system may also provide recommendations for improvement based on identified strengths and weaknesses.

Armed with this knowledge, businesses can refine their offerings and tailor their strategies to prioritize resources where it matters to strengthen their competitive advantage most efficiently and effectively.

Semantic Analysis

AI's capabilities extend beyond simple sentiment analysis and keyword extraction, delving into advanced techniques like semantic analysis and contextual understanding.

Semantic analysis refers to the examination and interpretation of the meaning and relationships of words, phrases, sentences, or documents within a given context. It involves the understanding of the underlying concepts, intentions, and semantics of language beyond their literal interpretation. These empower AI algorithms to grasp the nuanced meanings woven into review data, considering elements such as sarcasm, irony, and cultural context. By deciphering the intricacies of language, AI delves into the meaning and association of words and expressions. This contextual understanding enables businesses to identify not only explicit feedback but also the underlying emotions and motivations that drive consumer behavior.

Example

Here's a short example of semantic analysis and contextual understanding.

> Context: A conversation between two friends, Robert and Braulio, who are discussing their plans for the weekend.
>
> Robert: "I'm really excited about the concert tomorrow. I can't wait to see my favorite band perform live!"
>
> Braulio: "That's great! I wish I could join you, but I have a family gathering this weekend."

The semantic analysis focuses on understanding the meaning of the words used in the conversation and their relationship to each other. It involves deciphering the intent and extracting relevant information:

- Robert expresses excitement about the concert: The words "excited" and "can't wait" indicate his anticipation and enthusiasm for the upcoming event.
- Robert mentions seeing his favorite band perform live: This indicates his preference for a specific band and the desire to witness their live performance.

- Braulio expresses regret about not being able to join: Braulio acknowledges that he wishes to be part of the concert but is unable to attend due to a conflicting commitment.

Contextual understanding involves considering the broader context surrounding the conversation to gain a deeper understanding of the message being conveyed:

- Robert's excitement and anticipation imply that attending concerts and experiencing live music are significant interests or hobbies for him.
- Braulio's mention of a family gathering indicates the presence of a social obligation or commitment that takes precedence over attending the concert.

By applying semantic analysis and contextual understanding, we can comprehend the underlying meaning of the conversation, including Robert's enthusiasm for the concert and Braulio's regret about missing out due to a family event. We are now entering the space of predictive analytics as this knowledge gives us insight into how both Robert and Braulio may be influenced in future should we want to entice them for an event.

Predictive Analytics

AI's power in review data analysis extends beyond understanding and interpreting past reviews. By leveraging machine learning algorithms, AI can predict future outcomes and make personalized recommendations based on historical data. By analyzing patterns and trends in review data, AI algorithms can identify potential issues or emerging trends, enabling businesses to proactively address concerns or seize opportunities. Additionally, AI-powered recommendation systems can provide customers with tailored suggestions based on consumer preferences, past reviews, and behaviors, enhancing their overall experience and driving customer satisfaction.

Example

Jennifer is an online shopper who frequently purchases books from an e-commerce website. The website utilizes predictive analytics and recommendation systems to enhance her shopping experience.

By analyzing Jennifer's past purchase history, browsing behavior, and demographic information, predictive analytics provides insights into her future purchasing patterns. It identifies trends and predicts the likelihood of her buying certain types of books.

The predictive analytics system analyzes Jennifer's previous purchases and notices that she frequently buys mystery novels and historical fiction. Based on this analysis, it predicts that she is likely to be interested in a newly released mystery novel and recommends this to her.

The AI system also identifies that other users with similar interests to Jennifer have also enjoyed reading other genres or authors. Based on this information, the system recommends this to Jennifer as she visits the website or by personalized e-mail notifications. From here on, Jennifer's response to the promotion (does she buy the suggested book?) as well as her review of that alternative book provides feedback for the AI system to refine future recommendations.

In this way, the predictive analytics and recommendation systems work together to enhance her shopping experience by providing tailored suggestions which simultaneously enhance sales.

Personalization

In line with the example of Jennifer, AI systems can further unpack how individual consumers behave and automatically suggest or execute the right engagement to optimize guest satisfaction as well as sales to that consumer. This is already happening in the online retail space where constant personalized offerings are trigger based on browsing history and previous purchases. This can be further coupled with sentiment analysis to ensure that positive reviews trigger more of the specific product/brand and negative experiences would result in avoiding selling this to the individual consumer.

Depending on how AI systems can be coupled with individual consumer profiles at the service organization or potentially beyond (this depends on privacy considerations), the opportunities are exceptional as the AI system would better understand Jennifer's online shopping behavior than she does herself and be able to give her exactly what she wants even if she may not realize that she does.

In hospitality organizations, AI systems provide personalization opportunities especially to those Goliaths who, due to the sheer size of their operations, cannot personalize services effectively at present. Identifying the guest during the service encounter will then be key for this personalization of services to be able to take place.

Real-Time Monitoring

The real-time nature of AI allows businesses to monitor and analyze review data as it is generated, providing immediate feedback and actionable insights. Real-time monitoring and actionable insights are crucial for any business because they provide timely and relevant information that enables proactive decision making, efficient problem solving, and effective resource allocation. By continuously monitoring key metrics and receiving real-time updates, businesses can identify emerging trends, detect potential issues or opportunities, and take immediate action to address them. Without real-time monitoring and actionable insights, businesses may miss out on crucial information, leading to delayed responses, missed opportunities, and decreased competitiveness in an increasingly fast-paced and data-driven business landscape.

For instance, on a camping ground, AI can pick up on live social media postings that express dissatisfaction with the cleanliness of the toilet and shower facilities (most certainly, a CSF for camping grounds). It may then, on the day, decide to intensify the cleaning schedule to remedy this and avoid further negative fallout. Also, for event organizers, tourism attractions or other service businesses that deal with sensitive social carrying capacity (the point where visitor numbers get too high and impact negatively on the visitor experience), the AI can recommend a live stop for entry as it monitors online posts from visitors.

The Future of Reviews

As technology continues to advance, the landscape of customer feedback is set to evolve further with AI. This section will explore the future of reviews, focusing on the potential impact of AI-generated reviews and the rise in interactive experiences.

AI and machine learning technologies have made significant strides in recent years, enabling the generation of human-like text. This has led to the emergence of AI-generated reviews, which can be used to create more personalized and engaging customer feedback. However, this also raises concerns about the authenticity and trustworthiness of reviews, as it becomes more challenging to distinguish between genuine human feedback and AI-generated content.

As AI-generated reviews become more prevalent, businesses and review platforms will need to invest in advanced algorithms and techniques to detect and combat fake reviews. Ensuring the authenticity and credibility of reviews will be critical in maintaining consumer trust and upholding the value of customer feedback.

With the rise in virtual and augmented reality technologies, the future of reviews may also include more interactive and immersive experiences. Consumers could virtually experience products and services before making a purchase decision, allowing for more informed choices based on first-hand experiences. This could revolutionize the way reviews are created and consumed, adding a new dimension to customer feedback.

The growing popularity of voice assistants like Amazon Alexa, Google Assistant, and Apple Siri has led to a surge in voice-based interactions. In the future, consumers may increasingly rely on voice-based reviews to gather information about products and services. Businesses will need to adapt their review strategies to accommodate this shift in consumer behavior.

As technology advances, the integration of reviews across different platforms and devices will become more seamless. Consumers will have access to customer feedback from various sources, all in one place, making it even easier to make informed purchasing decisions. In the hospitality industry, summarizing reviews is an essential practice for both businesses and potential customers. Summarizing reviews involves condensing the key points and insights from various customer reviews into a concise format, highlighting the most critical information.

The future of reviews may also include real-time feedback, allowing businesses to receive and respond to customer feedback instantly. This can help businesses address customer concerns more efficiently, enhance customer satisfaction within the service experience, and drive continuous improvement more immediately.

Takeaways

AI's influence in review data analysis is unquestionable as it automates sentiment analysis, identifies CSFs, comprehends context, provides predictive analytics and personalization, and allows for real-time monitoring of service delivery. AI will enhance the ability for service organizations to use review data in a number of ways:

1. *Efficiency*: AI will automate the process of analyzing large volumes of reviews, saving time and resources compared to manual review analysis. With AI, businesses can quickly process and extract valuable insights from a vast amount of customer feedback.

2. *Accuracy*: AI-powered sentiment analysis algorithms can accurately classify the sentiment expressed in reviews, whether it's positive, negative, or neutral. This enables businesses to understand customer opinions at scale and identify areas that require attention or improvement.

3. *Actionability*: AI algorithms can not only extract meaningful information from reviews, such as common themes, trends, and specific customer preferences, but also suggest appropriate actions in real time.

4. *Personalization*: AI-driven recommendation systems can provide personalized suggestions based on individual preferences and purchase history. AI can analyze customer preferences and make tailored recommendations, improving the customer experience and increasing sales.

As AI system functionality continues to evolve at a rapid pace, there will be many more utilizations that we cannot see at this point in time;

however, it is certain that in many areas, it will provide more efficient, accurate, actionable, and personalized review opportunities.

Case Study: The AI-Driven Renaissance by GAIN

Imagine a world where every aspect of your hotel stay, from the pillow you sleep on to the room temperature, is perfectly tailored to suit your preferences. How can hospitality leaders interpret the plethora of guest preferences? Vincent Somsen, advisor to Hotels, Travel Tech, and DMOs at Growth Advisors International Network (GAIN), believes AI holds the answer. He believes the key to understanding guest preferences lies in advanced algorithms paired with instant data insights.

Vincent believes the hospitality sector is at a turning point. Modern times present extremely high customer expectations, and conventional methods of service delivery frequently fall short. Hotels are balancing operational effectiveness, guest experiences, and profitability. AI may seem to be just another technology buzzword for some; however, Vincent believes it provides the key to unmatched guest satisfaction and operational excellence from what he has seen at hospitality brands GAIN works with.

Unveiling the Challenges

Understanding the challenges is crucial before looking at AI solutions. Especially larger hotels struggle with a lack of personalization and this affects the guest experience negatively. Also, resource distribution is often a guessing game, and this results in operational inefficiencies. Finally, customer reviews play a crucial role in hotel performance; however, hotels find themselves frequently inundated by feedback across multiple platforms.

AI to the Rescue

GAIN's perspective is crystal clear: AI is not merely an automation tool; it provides a gateway to deeper understanding and agility in hospitality. The manifestations of this AI-driven revolution touch every facet of a guest's experience. Guests are increasingly seeking personalized experiences. Now, imagine when they walk into their room to find the room settings perfectly attuned to them: from lights dimmed to their liking, playlists echoing their favorite tunes, to ambient room temperatures set just right. This personalization is not crafted from thin air; it is the result of AI meticulously analyzing insights from guests' prior interactions and stays.

However, this personalization extends beyond the room settings. The booking process, often a hassle, becomes a breeze with AI's predictive capabilities. Before a guest even intimates their checkout, AI, analyzing behavioral cues, will forecast this and ensure occupancy and a seamless turnover for the next guest.

Similarly, the guest experience in facilities in the hotel, be it the spa, restaurant, or gym, can be optimized. AI's forecasting can pinpoint peak usage times, enabling efficient staff allocation to make sure that guests' needs are met with attentive service.

The feedback loop, an essential touch point, undergoes a transformative change with AI-powered sentiment analysis tools. These tools delve deep. They intelligently prioritize feedback that necessitates urgent attention, categorize underlying sentiments, and even craft suggested responses. Such proactive measures turn a potentially negative review into an opportunity to foster a strong guest relationship.

Operational tasks, often deemed mundane, get a facelift with the integration of Large Language Models (LLMs), like ChatGPT. These mechanisms automate routine tasks, from e-mail to schedule creation, freeing hotel staff to truly focus on what they do best: curate unforgettable experiences for guests.

Yet, for all this to come to fruition, a foundational step is essential: evaluating the symbiosis between AI and your current tech setup. Once this harmony is established, AI can seamlessly intermingle with both the front-of-house and back-of-house operations. Think about it: a guest's entire journey, from check-in to check-out, supercharged with AI's precision...

And, what's a hotel room in the modern age without a touch of tech luxury? Smart speakers become more than just devices; they morph into personal concierges. From reserving a table at the hotel's restaurant, setting wake-up alarms, to dishing out local touristy tips, all this is a mere voice command away.

Operational hiccups, like malfunctioning equipment, can sour a guest's experience. But AI's predictive maintenance capabilities ensure that such issues are nipped in the bud, way before a guest even notices.

Finally, in the dynamic world of hospitality, pricing can make or break a deal. With AI's data-driven insights, hotels can adopt dynamic pricing strategies, always staying a step ahead of the competition while ensuring their coffers aren't left wanting. By delving into a guest's historical data, preferences, and online behaviors, AI crafts personalized packages or offers, enticing them for yet another memorable stay, priced just right.

In essence, this AI-driven paradigm shift isn't just about enhancing operational efficiencies or boosting revenues; it's about reimagining guest experiences, one AI-crafted interaction at a time.

Final Thoughts

In an era where attention spans are dwindling, the key is to captivate, engage, and inspire the guest. GAIN's narrative does just that, and more importantly, it is rooted in hands-on expertise, offering a bespoke professional service pack tailored for the hospitality industry. This isn't mere rhetoric; it is being done and it is working. By urging the hospitality industry to envision a future where technology and human touch coalesce seamlessly, GAIN is not just painting a vision but curates the tools to realize it. As we traverse this exciting narrative, one truth emerges crystal clear: the future of hospitality isn't merely about better stays. It's about sculpting unforgettable memories, one AI-driven memory at a time.

CHAPTER 7

Conclusions

We hope that you enjoyed this journey through online reviews. We believe the story of David and Goliath is an eye-opener that size does not always matter and that at the heart of all the technological complexity lies a simple truth that people want to engage with people and be recognized as the unique individuals they are. This also made us expand on the fact that at the foundation of successful online review marketing lies a strong foundation of service excellence, driven by structures that empower service employees and a culture that puts the customer first.

Various methods of acquiring review data from online marketplaces, review aggregation websites, and social media platforms are outlined. Techniques such as data scraping, application programming interfaces (APIs), online surveys, and third-party platforms are explored for data collection. The storage, cleaning, and preprocessing of online data are addressed, along with ethical and privacy considerations. As much as we understand that the typical reader may not fully understand the technicality of such processes, we felt it was important to outline the key practices here to appreciate the opportunities of automated data collection.

To create meaningful insights, the collected data needs to be structured and analyzed. A range of data analysis techniques are introduced. These techniques include sentiment analysis, topic modeling, text classification, review summarization, time series analysis, and review clustering. Also here, we acknowledge that not every reader will fully understand the techniques and we have tried to keep things simple and straightforward. For the more technical-oriented reader, QR links are provided to explore additional information and examples.

We hope that you shared our excitement for the many marketing opportunities that avail themselves when you accept the paradigm that online review data contains the message of what your unique customers

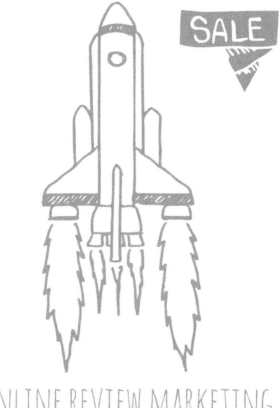

ONLINE REVIEW MARKETING

really want. This, we believe, is a truly undervalued space where a lot of business success can be achieved—from aligning product and service concepts, to better market positioning, powerful and authentic marketing communication and customer engagement, and effective pricing strategies. The discussion of the "economy of trust" reminds us of the importance of authenticity, transparency, and honesty in online review marketing and our customer engagements.

With AI, we can expect online review marketing to experience continued opportunities (and challenges). We do, however, believe that the core message of what we have presented in this book will not change. Principles such as service excellence, personalization, authenticity, transparency, and honesty will continue to be important and perhaps be even more important in driving business success.

Throughout the book, compelling case studies of organizations and companies that have implemented the proposed strategies are presented. These cases aim to inspire you to embark on similar initiatives, utilizing the authentic voice of your customers as a guiding force. Two themes that run through these cases are curiosity and humility–curiosity in terms of not being scared to change the status quo and humility to accept that we may not have gotten it right the first time around.

Do you own a business? We would be delighted to extend an invitation to you. If you're intrigued by this opportunity, kindly share your unique case study with us. There's a chance it could be highlighted prominently in online website or lectures or even included in the forthcoming edition of our book.

Scan the QR-code for more information about the fast-paced, interconnected world of online reviews.

Tips Using Review Data

1. *Collect data from multiple sources*: Gather review data from a variety of sources, such as social media platforms, online review sites, and customer surveys, to get a comprehensive view of customer sentiment.
2. *Analyze data in real time*: Use real-time analysis tools to identify trends and patterns in review data as they happen, so you can respond quickly to emerging issues.
3. *Identify key themes*: Use text analysis tools to identify key themes and sentiment across large sets of review data. This will help you identify areas for improvement and prioritize your efforts.
4. *Use review data for product development*: Use customer feedback to identify areas for improvement and develop new products or features that address customer needs and preferences.
5. *Monitor your competitors*: Monitor your competitors' review data to identify gaps in the market and stay ahead of emerging trends.

6. *Respond to customer feedback*: Respond to customer feedback in a timely and personalized manner to show customers that you value their feedback and are committed to addressing their concerns.

7. *Enhance your marketing*: Incorporate positive reviews into your marketing efforts, and use customer feedback to develop targeted advertising campaigns that resonate with your target audience.

8. *Measure the impact of review data*: Use metrics such as customer satisfaction, revenue, and brand reputation to measure the impact of review data on your business.

9. *Ensure the ethical use of review data*: Obtain consent from customers before using their review data, ensure that the data is anonymized to protect privacy, and use the data only for its intended purpose.

10. *Improve your review data strategy*: Review your review data strategy regularly, and look for ways to improve your data collection and analysis processes.

Set Up a Review Data Strategy in Five Steps

1. *Define* your goals: Before collecting and analyzing review data, it is important to define your goals. What are you hoping to achieve through this strategy? Are you looking to improve your products or services, increase customer satisfaction, or drive sales? Defining your goals will help you identify the metrics and data points that are most important to track.

2. *Choose* your review sources: Next, you'll need to decide which review sources to focus on. This could include social media platforms, online review sites, or customer surveys. Consider where your target audience is most likely to leave reviews and where you can gather the most valuable insights.

3. *Collect* and analyze the data: Once you have identified your review sources, it is time to start collecting and analyzing the data. This could involve using a review management tool to aggregate reviews from different sources and track key metrics such as sentiment, frequency, and ratings.

4. *Take* action based on insights: After analyzing the review data, it is important to take action based on the insights you have gathered.

This could involve addressing specific customer complaints or making changes to your products or services based on feedback.

5. *Monitor* and adjust your strategy: Finally, it is important to monitor and adjust your review data strategy over time. Keep track of key metrics and make adjustments as needed to ensure that you're meeting your goals and driving continuous improvement.

Several Companies That Can Support Your Needs

Trustpilot: Trustpilot is a leading review platform that allows businesses to collect and manage customer reviews. It offers a range of features, including review invitations, review analytics, and integration with other business tools.

Yelp: Yelp is a popular review platform that focuses on local businesses. It allows customers to leave reviews and ratings for businesses and offers a range of tools for businesses to manage their online reputation.

Google Reviews: Google Reviews is a review platform that is integrated with Google Maps and Google Search. It allows customers to leave reviews for businesses and offers businesses the ability to respond to reviews and manage their online presence.

TripAdvisor: TripAdvisor is a review platform that is focused on the travel industry. It allows customers to leave reviews and ratings for hotels, restaurants, and other travel-related businesses and offers businesses a range of tools to manage their online reputation.

G2 Crowd: G2 Crowd is a review platform that is focused on B2B software and services. It allows customers to leave reviews and ratings for software products and offers businesses the ability to manage their online reputation and generate leads.

Notes

Chapter 1

1. Anderson (2012).
2. TripAdvisor (2019).
3. McCollough and Bharadwaj (1992), pp. 148–155.

Chapter 2

1. Zeithaml, Beery, and Parasuraman (1996), pp. 31–46.
2. Zeithaml (1988), pp. 2–22.
3. Heskett, Jones, Loveman, Sasser, and Schlesinger (1994), pp. 164–174.
4. Jansen and Martin (2017), pp. 1–10.
5. Maslow (1943), pp. 370–396.
6. Reichheld (2006).

Chapter 5

1. Hensens, Sharrock, and Struwig (2020), pp. 18–26.
2. Reichheld (2006).
3. ABCNews (2019).
4. Amazon (2023).

References

ABCNews. 2019. "FTC Settles First-ever Lawsuit Involving Fake Online Retailer Reviews." https://abcnews.go.com/Business/ftc-settles-lawsuit-involving-fake-online-retailer-%20reviews/story?id=61354710.

Amazon. 2023. "Amazon Continues to Take Action Against Fake Review Brokers." www.aboutamazon.com/news/policy-news-views/amazon-continues-to-take-action-against-fake-review-brokers.

Anderson, C. 2012. The Impact of Social Media on Lodging Performance. Centre for Hospitality Research Publications. https://ecommons.cornell.edu/items/d64bbbba-651a-4e13-a058-af3e2e82f4cf.

Hensens, R., P.L. Sharrock, and M.C. Struwig. 2020. "Hotel Guest Experiences of Sustainable Practices." *Journal of Hospitality and Tourism Management* 45, pp. 1826.

Heskett, J.L., T.O. Jones, G.W. Loveman, W.E. Sasser and L.A. Schlesinger. 1994. "Putting the Service-profit Chain to Work." *Harvard Business Review* 72, no. 2, pp. 164174.

Jansen, B.J. and B. Martin. 2017. "Online Reputation Management: A Systematic Review of the Literature and Agenda for Future Research." *Journal of Business Research* 70, pp. 110.

Maslow, A.H. 1943. "A Theory of Human Motivation." *Psychological Review* 50, no. 4, pp. 370396. https://doi.org/10.1037/h0054346.

McCollough, M.A. and S.G. Bharadwaj. 1992. "The Recovery Paradox: An Examination of Consumer Satisfaction in Relation to Disconfirmation, Service Quality, and Attribution-based Theories." *Journal of Service Research* 1, no. 2, pp. 148155.

Reichheld, F.F. 2006. "The Ultimate Question: Driving Good Profits and True Growth." *Harvard Business Press.*

TripAdvisor. 2019. "Online Reviews Remain a Trusted Source of Information When Booking Trips, Reveals New Research." TripAdvisor. https://tripadvisor.mediaroom.com/2019-07-16-Online-Reviews-Remain-a-Trusted-Source-of-Information-When-Booking-Trips-Reveals-New-Research.

Zeithaml, V.A. 1988. "Consumer Perceptions of Price, Quality, and Value: A Means-end Model and Synthesis of Evidence." *Journal of Marketing* 52, no. 3, pp. 222.

Zeithaml, V.A., L.L. Berry and A. Parasuraman. 1996. "The Behavioral Consequences of Service Quality." *Journal of Marketing* 60, no. 2, pp. 3146.

About the Authors

Hans Keukenschrijver

With both a technical and commercial background, Hans has been involved in designing new solution–market combinations and pivoting business models in tech industries. He is an accomplished Dutch serial entrepreneur and CEO and co-owner of Olery, a company specialized in collecting, aggregating, normalizing, analyzing, and distributing reputation data in the travel industry.

Beyond his involvement with Olery, he actively contributes as a mentor and advisor to numerous startups in the Netherlands, leveraging his extensive experience and expertise to guide and nurture emerging businesses. Recognized for his profound knowledge in the realm of online reputation management and the hospitality industry, he frequently takes the stage as a speaker at industry events and conferences, sharing his insights and shedding light on crucial topics.

Hans loves to fantasize about new technologies, running, sailing with his family, and checking reviews before entering a restaurant.

Menno Beker

He is a successful Dutch entrepreneur, experienced executive, and co-owner of various companies, including Olery.com. With more than 25 years of expertise in the digital and reputation management space, he has developed a strong reputation himself.

His areas of specialization include hospitality, retail and e-commerce ecosystems, as well as marketing, where he has demonstrated his ability to create highly effective global digital strategies. He has been involved in multiple operational aspects throughout his career. Currently, together with Hans, he serves as an advisor and boardroom consultant for several businesses.

Additionally, he is a sought-after speaker at industry events and conferences, sharing his insights on topics such as online reputation management and the hospitality industry. He has also coauthored the Dutch book titled *Raak: Effectieve communicatie van informeren tot co-creëren.*

In addition to his entrepreneurial pursuits, he actively mentors and advises other startups. Furthermore, he has been a judge for various startup competitions, lending his expertise to identify and support emerging talent in the startup ecosystem.

Menno is in a relationship with Kim, a father of four boys, living a #fourboyscrazylife as Kim always mentioned, and he finds joy in skiing, sports, and cherishing the importance of friends.

Coauthor Dr. Wouter Hensens

Dr. Wouter Hensens is the Executive Dean of Stenden South Africa, a campus of NHL Stenden University of Applied Sciences in the coastal town of Port Alfred, South Africa. His doctoral research focused on the impact of online guest reviews on conventional hotel classification systems, and this started his journey in the study of online reviews.

His work includes the integration of online review data in hotel rating systems in Abu Dhabi, Qatar, Bahrain, and Sharjah and a number of publications on the nature and use of online review data. He loves to explore the true voice of the guest through the analysis of online review data and believes that online reviews will continue to shape the services sector for the better.

Wouter is married to Marin with two children, Lana and Alec and lives in the quaint town of Port Alfred, South Africa, where he also serves as the Chair of the Sunshine Coast Tourism Board. In his free time, he loves playing golf and experiencing unique hospitality concepts.

Index

OTHER TITLES IN THE TOURISM AND HOSPITALITY MANAGEMENT COLLECTION

Elizabeth Stringam, Editor

- *Talent Disruption* by Alexander Mirza
- *How a Global Pandemic Changed the Way We Travel* by Jacqueline Jeynes
- *Hotel Revenue Management* by Dave Roberts
- *Astrotourism* by Michael Marlin
- *Enhancing Joy in Travel* by Virginia Murphy-Berman
- *Healthy Vines, Pure Wines* by Pamela Lanier and Jessica Nicole Hughes
- *Overtourism* by Helene von Magius Møgelhøj
- *Food and Beverage Management in the Luxury Hotel Industry* by Sylvain Boussard
- *Targeting the Mature Traveler* by Jacqueline Jeynes
- *Hospitality* by Chris Sheppardson
- *A Time of Change in Hospitality Leadership* by Chris Sheppardson
- *Food and Architecture* by Subhadip Majumder and Sounak Majumder
- *Improving Convention Center Management Using Business Analytics and Key Performance Indicators* by Myles T. McGrane

Concise and Applied Business Books

The Collection listed above is one of 30 business subject collections that Business Expert Press has grown to make BEP a premiere publisher of print and digital books. Our concise and applied books are for...

- Professionals and Practitioners
- Faculty who adopt our books for courses
- Librarians who know that BEP's Digital Libraries are a unique way to offer students ebooks to download, not restricted with any digital rights management
- Executive Training Course Leaders
- Business Seminar Organizers

Business Expert Press books are for anyone who needs to dig deeper on business ideas, goals, and solutions to everyday problems. Whether one print book, one ebook, or buying a digital library of 110 ebooks, we remain the affordable and smart way to be business smart. For more information, please visit www.businessexpertpress.com, or contact sales@businessexpertpress.com.

Printed in the USA
CPSIA information can be obtained
at www.ICGtesting.com
LVHW021747311024
795349LV00002B/236